THE SOUND AND THE GLORY

THE SOUND
AND THE GLORY

HOW THE SEATTLE SOUNDERS SHOWED
MAJOR LEAGUE SOCCER HOW TO WIN OVER AMERICA

MATT PENTZ

Published by ECW Press
665 Gerrard Street East
Toronto, Ontario, Canada M4M 1Y2
416-694-3348 / info@ecwpress.com

Editor for the Press: Michael Holmes
Cover design: Michel Vrana
Author photo: © Amanda Snyder

LIBRARY AND ARCHIVES CANADA CATALOGUING
IN PUBLICATION

Pentz, Matt, author
    The sound and the glory : how the Seattle
Sounders showed Major League Soccer how to
win over America / Matt Pentz.

Issued in print and electronic formats.
ISBN 978-1-77041-462-4 (softcover)
ISBN 978-1-77305-324-0 (PDF)
ISBN 978-1-77305-323-3 (EPUB)

    1. Seattle Sounders FC (Soccer team)—
History. 2. Soccer teams—Washington (State)—
Seattle—History. I. Title.

GV943.6.S43P45 2019   796.334'6309797772
C2018-905289-9   C2018-905290-2

PRINTED AND BOUND IN CANADA

PRINTING: MARQUIS   5   4   3   2   1

PREFACE

On the afternoon of November 13, 2007, a group of soccer fans stood shoulder to shoulder at the George & Dragon pub in the Seattle neighborhood of Fremont. The occasion was a badly kept secret: the city was to be granted an expansion franchise to become the 15th team in North America's top professional division, Major League Soccer.

The mood was festive. Despite the lunchtime hour, Boddingtons, Guinness and local favorite Manny's Pale Ale flowed freely. Drew Carey, the game show host and new team's celebrity co-owner, bought a round of beers for the standing-room-only crowd.

Adrian Hanauer, though, was unquestionably the man of the hour.

A local businessman whose family owned a successful bedding manufacturing company, Hanauer dated his soccer fandom to the first time he caught a glimpse of the North American Soccer League Sounders at the age of eight in the '70s. He became the managing partner of a minor-league iteration of the club in 2002, an investment so shaky he once convinced his players to begrudgingly take pay cuts just to keep the team solvent.

In this moment, in 2007, scanning a sea of beaming faces, that initial sacrifice was worth it.

Few patrons were aware how close Hanauer had been to landing an MLS franchise two years earlier — and that he viewed the delay as a blessing in disguise.

For most of the 2000s, the league stood on trembling legs. In 2002, it contracted two of its 12 teams, the Miami Fusion and Tampa Bay Mutiny. The U.S. men's national team's run to the World Cup quarterfinals that same year inspired a brief uptick in interest, but when Hanauer submitted his first expansion bid in 2005, he did so with trepidation. When the league went with Salt Lake City instead, Hanauer reacted partially with disappointment but with an underlying sense that it was for the best. In the minor leagues, at least operating costs were lower. At the time, MLS was a risky bet.

A decade on from that announcement at the George & Dragon, Hanauer's club and the league he eventually joined were almost unrecognizable. By 2016, Major League Soccer boasted 22 teams, with a second Los Angeles club on the way and a Miami franchise theoretically in the offing. MLS HQ proudly unveiled a list of 10 cities competitively bidding for the final four slots in what the league said would ultimately settle at 28. Commissioner Don Garber's oft-stated goal of becoming an internationally relevant league remained outlandish but was no longer incomprehensible.

If the world's game hadn't yet broken into mainstream American consciousness, professional soccer was on steadier ground on these shores than ever before. In many ways, it had Hanauer's Seattle Sounders to thank. The Sounders, along with the Toronto FC team that was part of the same wave of expansion, created a blueprint that every successful new franchise since has borrowed.

Whereas the original clubs catered to a suburban crowd, building youth practice fields next to no-frills stadiums in an attempt to draw in soccer moms, Seattle played in the heart of its city. It catered to and worked with its most dedicated fans, cultivating a supporters' culture that was at the time rare in MLS. By sharing business operations with the NFL's Seahawks, the club was lent immediate credibility.

The payoff resulted in attendance figures that would be the envy of teams even in the biggest leagues in the world. The Sounders averaged more than 42,000 fans per home game in 2016, the second-largest figure in the Western Hemisphere and in the top 35 internationally — topping juggernauts such as Chelsea in England and AC Milan in Italy.

Yet as the club continued to mature, Hanauer wanted more. Midway through the 2016 season, he and the Sounders brass began drawing up ambitious plans to sell out the entirety of CenturyLink Field within the next decade. Timed around what they hoped would be a United-States-co-hosted 2026 World Cup, Seattle aimed to fill all 67,000 seats for every game, which would vault it comfortably into the top 10 in the world.

Before those grand plans came to fruition, though, the Sounders needed to finally win it all.

For all of the club's early, consistent success, Seattle had yet to actually win the league. There was a sense that its grand project was stagnating. Buzz around the city had flatlined, its sports fans tiring of the team that reached the postseason annually only to fall short every year.

To reach Hanauer's lofty goals — and drag MLS into heights even Garber might marvel at — the Sounders needed the jolt of a championship.

To get there would require the kind of tumult a club previously built on stability had never known, a power struggle over the present and future of the franchise. To get there would take firing the only coach Seattle's modern era had ever known — and a title run so unlikely it could have hardly been scripted.

ONE

Sɪɢɪ Sᴄʜᴍɪᴅ sᴀᴛ ɪɴ silence in his cluttered office, staring blankly out the window when not looking down at hands creased with age.

The walls of the room were covered with photos of sweaty, jubilant soccer players, most of them lifting one silver trophy or another. To look up would mean coming to grips with all he'd accomplished here and, by extension, what he had just lost. To look up would be an admission that it was over.

The old coach had been fired once before, by his hometown L.A. Galaxy. This felt more personal, somehow. The hollow ache in his chest was more repressive than he remembered.

Seattle was supposed to be his legacy, the exclamation point on a long and storied career. In seven previous campaigns, starting with the Major League Soccer expansion season of 2009, Schmid's Sounders never once missed the playoffs. They won four U.S. Open Cups, not the league championships they craved but trophies nevertheless.

Seattle's off-field gains started with the consistent success the winningest coach in MLS history built from scratch. Yet the ultimate triumph proved elusive. To fans weaned on steady victories, the shortcomings grew more unacceptable with each passing year.

Festering frustration came to a head in the summer of 2016, midway through a season during which everything that could have gone wrong had.

After a decision that felt simultaneously abrupt and a long time coming, Schmid found himself on the wrong end of an early-morning phone call informing him of his termination. Sitting in what was now his former office, he peered out the window as the team that was no longer his walked out to practice without him.

Schmid pulled his phone out of his pocket, checked its blank face for what he hoped was an update on his ride and sighed. A gentle knock disturbed his brooding. Nicolas Lodeiro walked in with his hand outstretched before pulling Schmid in close for a hug.

"I'll do everything I can to help make the playoffs, take on any role," Lodeiro promised, prescient if a few days late to save the coach's job. "I've come here to win titles."

His boldness drew a resigned smile from Schmid: "You've come to the right place."

Schmid had personally helped recruit Seattle's new star. He'd coached the player's previous coach in Columbus back in the day, and in this business, personal touches like that could make all the difference. Lodeiro, he was sure, would turn the season around. He was the missing piece. The timing of Lodeiro's addition as an impact midseason signing was an unfortunate coincidence. That Schmid was somehow still in the building upon his arrival was considerably more awkward.

Out in the hallway, visibly uncomfortable with this exchange of pleasantries, stood general manager Garth Lagerwey. This was supposed to be a cleaner break. Lagerwey hadn't spared a thought to how it would look if the coach's ride was running late.

For a franchise often regarded as MLS's model of stability, the overlap was illustrative. Seattle's past and future eras collided often that summer, but rarely as clumsily as they did that morning. Lagerwey finally had the control he had long desired, but the transition was never going to be as straightforward as he'd hoped.

For once in his life, Lagerwey's timing was off. As such, the collision course between him and Schmid was inevitable from the outset.

When Lagerwey was hired as GM, in the winter of 2015 and away from Salt Lake, the Sounders were coming off the most successful year in their history. A few bounces the other way, and Seattle could've become the first team in league history to sweep all three major trophies in a single season. Coming in as an interloper from the outside, Lagerwey did not find an especially eager audience at staff meetings. And why would he?

Schmid was open to collaboration, more so than most of his detractors knew. Longevity like his demanded adaptability. Building trust and gaining his ear, though, took time. The coach still set the tone during meetings, and his voice carried the weight of the last word.

So far, the system had worked. Seattle's brain trust experienced only sustained success from year one. Even if they hadn't yet summited the loftiest peak, in the winter and spring of 2015 the breakthrough felt inevitable.

"It was stupid," Lagerwey said, "to take the job when I did."

Of all the adjectives used to describe the general manager, not even his biggest critics often reach for *stupid*. Even they would allow that despite his faults, Lagerwey possessed one of the sharpest minds in North American soccer. One does not jump directly from the Miami Fusion's bench into Georgetown law school without a seriously keen intellect. From Georgetown came a spell as an attorney at Latham & Watkins, the world's highest-billing law firm. The work was as punishing — up to 100 hours a week — as it was lucrative. Lagerwey would later regard his time in corporate law as the formative experience of his life.

Still, seven years after his goalkeeping career ended with the indignity of a roster cut, Lagerwey wasn't entirely content. He wanted back into the world of professional sports. His big break came over Christmas 2006, wrapped in the unlikely present of a request to work through the holidays. The case involved working closely with Dave Checketts, the owner of both the NHL's St. Louis Blues and MLS's Real Salt Lake. The latter connection especially piqued Lagerwey's interest — particularly once RSL hired Jason Kreis, his best friend and former Duke teammate, as its head coach early the next year.

"Life, to some degree, is about luck and timing," Lagerwey said.

That September, Lagerwey signed on as RSL's general manager. He could have hardly scripted a better situation within which to hone his new craft. He and Kreis inherited a club just a few years into its existence and perennially among the dregs of the league. Expectations were low, allowing them to experiment freely and churn through players with abandon. By the time both men left Salt Lake, the small-market club had won the MLS Cup, played in another title game and reached the final of the CONCACAF Champions League.

So for all Lagerwey was willing to sit back and observe early on in his Sounders tenure, eventually his confidence in his ideas and willingness to share them won out over decorum.

A heavyset man with a booming voice, Lagerwey filled every room he entered. He had a knack for remembering personal details from even the briefest encounters with strangers; he also had a tendency to dominate conversation. He's the type of sports executive you would like to grab a beer with: a native of the Chicago suburbs, Lagerwey once proudly traded his typical business casual for a Cubs jersey on the sidelines of a training session that overlapped with the World Series.

The contrast with his predecessor was jarring to those accustomed to the front office's status quo. Hanauer was the general manager from the club's inception until late 2014, when the majority owner stepped aside to concentrate on the business side of the organization. Soft-spoken and bookish in his wire-rimmed glasses, Hanauer could hardly be more different in personality from the boisterous Lagerwey.

"Adrian is a really good listener," Schmid said, the subtext nodding toward Lagerwey obvious. "He'll listen. He'll take it in and contemplate it. I think Adrian and I knew what lane to stay in. That didn't mean you didn't comment on the other guy's greater area of expertise, and you offered your opinion. But at the end, you knew that that was his decision-making lane."

With Lagerwey in the fold, responsibilities were less delineated. The 2015 season fell apart in the span of a few hours midway through June, and tension ratcheted up behind the scenes. Star forward Obafemi Martins left a fateful Open Cup match against rival Portland on a stretcher with a groin injury that cost him two months. Later in that same game, Clint Dempsey ripped up the referee's notebook in protest and picked up a suspension. Without its two best players, Seattle cratered, losing eight of 10 matches. Every defeat increased the strain.

There wasn't an obvious flashpoint in the struggle for power between Schmid and Lagerwey, narratively convenient as that would have been. It played out more as a cold war, distrust creeping between two successful men tasked with leading the franchise.

In his corner, Lagerwey retreated to the places he often sought when confronted with a complex problem.

When he first went back to school, Lagerwey would doze off between the wood-paneled bookshelves of Georgetown's law library after just a few hours of studying. As a professional athlete, his body had grown accustomed to stimuli in short, intense bursts. He was forced to retrain his brain. Later, at Latham & Watkins, he pushed himself to levels he never would have imagined.

"I learned certain things," Lagerwey said. "After 45 straight hours, my cognitive abilities would decline. You stop being able to do simple things easily. You never thought you would discover that point. Maybe at a bar."

He marveled at the style of management that would drive subordinates to their respective breaking points. Sure, the fat checks paid out every other week served as plenty of motivation, but Lagerwey also grew to deeply respect the executives in their corner offices for their ability to inspire.

"It wasn't fun," Lagerwey said. "Like, it might be intellectually interesting to explore. *I can no longer read this note in front of me. My brain is shutting down.* But from that, I learned so much and actually had so many good experiences."

As such, Lagerwey didn't always have a lot of patience for players and colleagues either unwilling or unable to push themselves toward those outer limits. The former attorney spoke often about applying the lessons he learned in corporate law to professional sports. That could involve an increased reliance on analytics produced by Seattle's well-regarded sports science staff. It manifested itself in buzzwords like *empowerment* and *accountability*.

There was a detached lack of sentimentality to it as well. Lagerwey purposefully kept himself at a slight remove from his players to avoid emotion clouding his judgment. Having been blooded in such a cutthroat environment, he did not shy away from making the tough calls, even when — or perhaps especially when — they involved veterans beloved both by teammates and fans.

"That's the job. You have to be able to do that," Lagerwey said. "Some of those decisions are even going to be unpopular internally."

Internally might have referred to the delicate chemistry of the locker room. It could also have meant the cramped coaches' meeting space a few doors down.

The Sounders dragged themselves into the playoffs once more in 2015, but they didn't stay long. A younger, ascendant FC Dallas team ran rings around them for the better part of their two-game Western Conference semifinal. Seattle was eliminated on penalty kicks. Familiar grumbling increased in volume. And within the club hierarchy, divisions deepened.

As rewarding as professional sport could be, financially and otherwise, it was also a brutal workplace. Even when the ax was about to drop, the athlete didn't always sense it swinging down.

Chad Barrett drove to the team's practice facility in late 2015 optimistic that his Sounders contract would be renewed for another year. The journeyman forward had been reasonably productive in spot duty during the season that'd just ended. Considering his age and experience, the $10,000 raise he was due on his $100,000 salary was paltry by MLS standards.

The leaves were falling ahead of the coming winter when he pulled into a sparsely populated lot. The cars he parked next to unnerved him. End-of-season meetings were typically called in waves. Players on their way out were often brought in earliest. So when Barrett spotted several automobiles that belonged to expensive veterans he knew were in danger of being cut, he felt a cold chill.

Barrett had known Schmid since he was a teenager. Schmid coached the U.S. under-20 team at the 2005 World Youth Championship, during which Barrett scored the goal that felled an Argentina team led by an up-and-coming prospect named Lionel Messi.

When Barrett considered signing with the Sounders prior to the 2014 season, Schmid didn't sugarcoat it: With Dempsey and Martins ahead of him on the depth chart, playing time was likely to be sparse. If he was willing to take and embrace a complementary role, though, he was more than welcome.

"He's the most honest coach I ever played for," Barrett said of Schmid. "I felt like I could trust everything that came out of his mouth."

What came out of Schmid's mouth that morning in his office was unexpected and unpleasant: "I don't want to waste your time. We've got to let you go."

Barrett slumped down the hall for an even briefer meeting with Lagerwey. The player could stay if he agreed to a significant pay cut, which he quickly declined. Sitting across the desk from the man he was convinced made the decision to let him go, Barrett seethed in his leather chair. He also privately wondered how differently it might have gone if Hanauer were still in charge.

"With Adrian, it didn't seem like he was scheming," Barrett said. "With Garth, you never really knew what he was up to. You can't really form any kind of relationship. I didn't have a relationship with Garth."

The unemotional approach Lagerwey deemed necessary grated at Schmid, driving a further wedge into their working relationship.

To some degree, head coaches and general managers are inherently, inescapably at odds. At the risk of oversimplification, coaches live in the short term, surviving from week to week. General managers must take a longer view. It's subjective versus objective, hands on versus at arm's length.

"I'm not in the locker room most days, and nor should I be, in my opinion," Lagerwey said. "My job is to be thinking strategically about how we do things for the next five to seven years. The coach and the general manager have fundamentally different jobs."

When it came to building a team, those fundamental differences clashed. Coaches tended to trust players more as they aged.

In a high-stress job in which either success or failure is written in bold on the scoreboard every week, there was a tendency to lean on veterans you knew you could trust. At the other end of the spectrum, general managers valued players less as they got older. Removed from the guts and gore of the week-to-week grind, when viewed on a spreadsheet, Lagerwey would always rather his teams skew younger.

"Older players, by definition, their production is going to decline at some point," Lagerwey said. "And you tend to be paying them more. Players are assets when you talk about trades and building your team. You have to use them efficiently."

Sitting in the coaches' box at CenturyLink Field looking down over his charges in early 2017, Lagerwey asked what was at first a puzzling question: are you a *Game of Thrones* fan?

Lamar Neagle, a popular winger who with Barrett was part of that first wave of Sounders veterans to be culled during Lagerwey's tenure, was a hometown kid from nearby Federal Way. The winger was active in the community and often the friendly face the club sent out to photo ops with diehard fans. His wife, Natalie, was also from the area, and she survived a public health scare during the 2014 playoffs that further endeared the couple to fans. They put a positive spin on his trade to D.C. United, at least at first — at least until she found out she was pregnant shortly after they moved into their new apartment across the country from their families.

Looking back now and with the same unshakable sunniness with which he approaches just about everything, Lagerwey offered only a bemused shrug. Business was business, Neagle was getting older, and he needed the cap space.

Are you a *Game of Thrones* fan? You know the kill list of enemies Arya Stark read before she went to bed?

"I bet you anything I'm on the list of names Lamar Neagle reads from every night," Lagerwey said while keeping his eyes on the match playing out below. "You can't go through this job worrying about being liked, because that's not going to happen."

The kicker: a few months after that conversation in the coaches' box, Lagerwey traded with D.C. to bring Neagle back to Seattle — at the far lesser price of a fourth-round draft pick than the valuable allocation money D.C. used to acquire him.

Business was business.

Schmid's final off-season in Seattle was troubled from the start. It wasn't even certain that he would return for 2016 after that discouraging Dallas defeat until Lagerwey let the news slip during a forum with Sounders season-ticket holders.

"Let me put something to bed: Sigi is our coach. Sigi will be our coach. Sigi is my coach," Lagerwey told the crowd that November, a public expression of solidarity that would crumble over the next nine months. The general manager then called out to the coach, who was sitting discreetly in the back of the darkened Paramount Theatre: "Sigi, you cool with being partners another year?"

Schmid nodded in assent, but judging from his sheepish, puzzled initial reaction, no one had bothered to give him a heads-up about the announcement beforehand. Nor had anyone notified his players, either, many of whom were also in the audience and none of whom had been asked their opinion on whether Schmid should be retained.

"No one had any idea," longtime Sounders captain Brad Evans recalled of the bizarre exchange. "I think all the guys behind the scenes were thinking, '*What just happened?*'"

Barely a fortnight before the new campaign, another ominous sign came. Martins had been offered a deal with a club in the Chinese Super League that stood to nearly double his annual salary, and he intended to take it. His departure left a hole that nobody else on the roster could fill — and widened the fissure between Schmid and Lagerwey.

It was another clash of short-term pressure versus long-term planning. In MLS, new players could be added only during two stretches of the calendar, during a chunk of spring and again in late summer. After his team opened the season with three consecutive losses, and perhaps sensing a dark hand creeping over his shoulder, Schmid and the coaching staff pushed for an influential acquisition sooner rather than later.

Yet one could hardly blame Lagerwey for dragging his feet. MLS roster rules allowed for three players whose contracts counted only as a minor hit against the salary cap. Those slots, reserved for the biggest stars, could make or break you. Martins's abrupt departure had left little time to scout and negotiate with potential replacements. In addition, with most of the South American and European leagues building to a climax in the spring, the majority of the best players are typically available only in the summer.

In the meantime, losses piled up. This was an inopportune moment for what was shaping up to be the worst year since the team joined MLS. In the background, Hanauer and the higher-ups were carefully crafting their ambitious plans for the future. It was crucial to maintain momentum, not forestall it.

"Everybody could sense that there was tension," Evans said. "I think the guys who were playing for Sigi resented the new GM, because guys were used to getting what they wanted whenever they wanted it. Now there was somebody telling them 'no.' There was pushback, and things kind of went into a tailspin from there. The team wasn't doing well, whether that's because subconsciously you could sense there was unrest in the club or because we just weren't scoring goals.

"The tension just builds and builds. I have a really close relationship with Sigi. I can tell when there's something going on. I pick up on cues in rooms that other guys, the younger guys, would never notice — whether that's the way one guy is sitting, or that they're not looking at each other during meetings. I pick up on all of those cues. It was like that for like a year."

Everything came to a head in late July in Kansas City, where the Sounders landed in the midst of a Midwestern heat wave. On-field temperatures topped out near 106 degrees Fahrenheit, coupled with humidity that thickened the air into soup. Especially compared with mild Seattle, conditions were oppressive. Spirits weren't helped by the midweek Open Cup elimination to Los Angeles a few days earlier, when the Sounders twice gave away leads via unforced individual errors.

Schmid visualized a locker room split in thirds: players who were squarely in his corner, those who weren't and guys floating somewhere in between. Even at the breaking point, he didn't sense an internal shift, and most of his players backed him on that. Still, morale was low. Seattle sat seven points out of the playoffs and was sinking fast.

Several players have described the playing conditions that afternoon in Kansas City as being as adverse as any they'd ever played in, including Evans, who grew up playing beneath a desert sun in Phoenix. The relentless heat was so exhausting that midway through the second half, defender Chad Marshall genuinely thought he was going to lose control of his bowels on national television.

"I was close," Marshall said. "The second water break in the second half kind of saved me. You're so tired that you just start to lose control."

Seattle lost 3–0, finishing one late consolation strike from becoming the first MLS team to ever go a full game without registering a single shot. The ESPN audience — and those sitting in air-conditioned owners' boxes — didn't have a sense for the searing heat. Few were aware of the extenuating circumstances.

To them, the Sounders looked like a team that quit on its coach.

The Tuesday morning after the Kansas City loss, Schmid woke up with an uneasy feeling. "I'm getting fired today," he told his wife, Valerie, and sure enough, the call informing him of his termination arrived shortly afterward. Schmid headed to the practice facility to address his team for the last time, then sat down in his office to wait for a ride back downtown.

Lodeiro, the missing piece, stuck his head in. They spoke through a translator; the Uruguayan again elicited a wry smile when he joked that the old coach really should learn Spanish. Even all things considered, Schmid got a kick out of how their chance meeting made Lagerwey squirm. Already, the general manager's best-laid plans had encountered an awkward hitch.

Standing in front of a semicircle of news cameras half an hour later, Hanauer spoke first. The firing of Schmid, and the naming of Brian Schmetzer as his interim replacement, the majority owner said multiple times, was his decision and his decision alone. Lagerwey stepped in next. Somberness did not come naturally to him, and he barely concealed his excitement at taking control.

"I did my best to be deferential, if anything, over these past 18 months," Lagerwey said. "This team doesn't play like any team I've ever built before. I'm looking forward to a new beginning."

The Schmid era held an exalted place in the soccer history of a city not lacking in it. Dating all the way back to the original NASL, the coach stood out as a figurehead as important as any this proud club had ever possessed.

That morning at the team facility, though, as past and future bumped headlong into one another, it was evident that the page had irrevocably turned.

TWO

WHAT IS IT ABOUT Seattle that makes it such a good soccer town?

That question had been posed and parsed ad nauseam since the Sounders took Major League Soccer by storm starting in 2009. The inquiry was natural, given the immensity of Seattle's early successes. For a time there, it *more than doubled* the second-place finisher in the MLS annual attendance rankings.

Reasons for soccer's popularity in the region, however, were not so easy to explain in just a sentence or two. There was no single magic bullet, as handy as that might have been. Plenty of plaudits were rained upon the collective wisdom of the Sounders' ownership group, and justifiably so. They hit all the right notes from the outset: identifying the right target audience, tapping into the city's countercultural vibe, compiling a talented roster from the jump. Importantly, though, the modern-day Sounders hit the scene at a critical juncture in Seattle's sporting history.

The NBA's Sonics had been cruelly wrested away to Oklahoma City in 2008, one year prior to the Sounders' debut. The politics of the relocation provided insight into the region as a whole. Seattle had actually come close to losing both MLB's

Mariners and the NFL's Seahawks during the early part of the previous decade, keeping them only by agreeing to publicly fund two shiny new stadiums side by side just south of downtown.

(A quick little aside: CenturyLink Field might never have been built if not for the efforts of the local soccer community. Despite not having obtained any assurances from MLS, the building was pitched as a two-sport venue for the Seahawks and a to-be-determined soccer tenant in order to broaden popular support. The ordinance passed but only narrowly, and many credited the soccer folks with getting it over the line.)

By the late 2000s, however, when the Sonics wanted in on the action, there was little appetite for another public subsidy to fund yet another sports palace. Besides, KeyArena itself had been renovated in the mid-'90s. What did it need another drastic facelift for? And the Sonics wouldn't actually leave, would they? They did, taking a pair of transcendent talents in Kevin Durant and Russell Westbrook with them.

For all of Seattle's rapid, tech-industry-fueled growth since the turn of the millennium, marooned out in the northwest corner of the country, it retained self-consciousness about its place in mainstream America. The loss of a big-league franchise was a serious blow to the city's collective psyche.

Nor did the other local teams offer much of a respite. That September, the Mariners earned the ignominious designation of becoming the first team in baseball history to spend more than $100 million on its payroll and lose at least a hundred games. The proud University of Washington football team finished winless, 0-12. Even the Seahawks won just four games, the future glories of the Pete Carroll era still a few years away.

Seattle was crying out for a winner, any winner. It was paramount, then, that the Sounders hit the ground running. If they were going to take advantage of the vacuum created by the Sonics' departure, they needed to be good, and they needed to be good right away.

Goalkeeper Kasey Keller, who had grown up just down the road in Olympia but made his name in Europe's biggest leagues, had agreed to come home as one of the club's first marquee signings for just such an opportunity. Keller played in the English Premier League, in the German Bundesliga and in multiple World Cups with the U.S. national team, but rarely had he ever experienced the nerves he felt jumping around in his belly prior to Seattle's inaugural match against the New York Red Bulls on March 19, 2009. Keller felt the anticipation building around the city in the days leading up to the match but knew how fleeting it could be.

"I felt a huge amount of pressure not to have those fans go home disappointed," Keller told me. "This is what we wanted. We want that relevancy. The last thing we wanted them to do was say, 'Meh,' to have that blasé feeling of, 'This is what the hype was all about? The team goes and gets their butts kicked, and who really cares?'"

With a festive crowd of 32,608 on hand, Sounders midfielder Fredy Montero scored the first goal of the club's modern era just 12 minutes in. The crafty Colombian assisted on Evans's tally that made it 2–0 on the other side of halftime and set the final score at 3–0 with another goal 15 minutes from the final whistle. Seattle won its first three MLS matches in quick succession, setting the tone for a season that, against precedent and league-wide expectation, ended in a playoff berth.

"Momentum was built because we were relevant from day one," Keller said. "There was an excitement based on it not only because of the expansion, but because of the atmosphere we created. It was such a perfect storm between so many influences, and we felt like we weren't going to let down our part of it on the field. If we hadn't been any good, definitely I don't think we would have had the momentum we built."

As Keller alluded, the expansion was a success on multiple fronts. Partnering with the Seahawks for business operations proved vital. While most of the franchises around MLS at the time could have been charitably described as amateurish, the NFL team's infrastructure gave the Sounders a professional sheen.

When asking the question posed in the first line of the chapter, many skeptics — especially those from a few hours down the road in Portland — wondered why the minor-league iterations of the Sounders had drawn so poorly. Even Brian Schmetzer's 2005 and 2007 USL champions, led by a proud local son and stocked with talent drawn mostly from the region, were lucky to attract a few thousand fans to home matches, tops.

"This is a major-league city," said Gary Wright, the long-time Seahawks VP who spearheaded the Sounders' transition to MLS, by way of explanation. "They didn't draw great as a minor-league team, but no minor-league team does. It's a mind-set."

It was vital, then, that the Sounders lived up to the *Major League* part of MLS. Thanks in no small part to the Seahawks' helping hands, from marketing to ticket sales to in-game promotions to the venue itself, the club was able to check all of those boxes in a way that few peers had ever matched.

Take, for example, game-day presentation. Back then, MLS teams used only a limited portion of the field for the pregame buildup, if they did so at all. The Sounders/Seahawks team thought bigger, always: cover the whole surface with flags and banners, shoot pillars of fire from behind the goalposts, thrill the senses.

"You've got to make it an event, a spectacle," Wright said. "From the business side, you can't control the wins and losses — other than spending money. You *can* control the experience, from the time fans come in the gates to the time they leave the gates. Control as much as you possibly can."

Things didn't always go off without a hitch. During a trial run the day before the opener against the Red Bulls, a pair of doves was released from the end line as part of the kickoff ceremony — only to be immediately preyed upon by a pair of hawks that lived up in the stadium's rafters. One dove careened into the fiberglass windows of the suite level with a thud. Another was carried off in the talons of one of the hawks. The dove idea was scrapped, but it was emblematic of a brain trust willing to push the envelope, and although they watched with horror as that poor bird was torn apart, they were not discouraged.

The Sounders also, importantly, homed in on a fruitful target demographic. It's helpful here to divide the brief history of the league into distinct iterations. Out of economic necessity as well as faulty targeting, the first generation of soccer-specific stadiums was built out in the suburbs rather than city centers. MLS 1.0 was designed to be family friendly — bring your kids out for a wholesome Sunday afternoon and let them run around while parents enjoy the match. The problem was, glorified day cares do not inspire brand loyalty.

"They were never going to buy season tickets for 18 games," Wright said. "To me, that was a bad idea right away."

By the time the league reached its third decade of existence, a clear divide had formed between the founding franchises and the clubs that came along later. First impressions made all the difference, and even consistent winners struggled to reorient their brands and regain their cities' respective interest. Kansas City was an instructive outlier, where a name change and move to one of the league's premier venues allowed it a fresh start.

Otherwise, the originals foundered. For the 2016 campaign, the bottom five teams in average attendance (Columbus, D.C., Colorado, Chicago and Dallas) had all been around since the inaugural season.

If MLS 1.0 was the era of suburbia, of half-empty stadiums and failed first impressions, the page was turned toward the middle of the last decade, first by Toronto, which made its debut in 2007 and whose blueprint Seattle's ownership group carefully pored over, and the Sounders themselves.

BMO Field, built along the shores of Lake Ontario, and CenturyLink Field both stood close to their respective city cores.

Both Toronto's and Seattle's ambitious ownership groups cultivated fan bases that skewed younger, trendier, looking for an alternative to the traditional North American professional sports teams. Wright wanted the folks who packed inside the George & Dragon for early-morning English Premier League matches.

"So many of those people probably weren't even really sports fans, but they were looking for some kind of outlet," Wright said.

Thus begat the stereotype, neither fair nor completely without basis, of the Sounders as a social club as much as a sporting institution. It was inclusive, hip, allowing supporters to feel a part of something bigger than themselves. In a city increasingly made up of transplants, that idea held appeal.

If Toronto paved the way, so did TFC fail in the other half of the equation early on: win-loss record. The Reds wouldn't qualify for the postseason for the first time until 2015, year nine. The Sounders, as mentioned already and in stark contrast, never once missed out. They were the complete package.

The payoff was striking. At a time when most MLS contemporaries considered 20,000 fans a runaway success, Seattle shattered the ceiling. The Sounders enjoyed nearly 31,000 in average attendance during its inaugural campaign, and the numbers kept climbing from there. They didn't start to tail off until after 2013, when they had gone north of 44,000 — with a one-off high of 66,216, four home matches that topped 50,000 and an average that victory-lapped the closest challenger.

Still, for as much praise as the Sounders' ownership group, transition team and support staff have deservedly collected over the years, the factors laid out here don't tell the whole story. Those extraordinary figures were not, could not, be the result of fortuitous timing, slick marketing and well-oiled ops alone. For the rest, one must dig a little deeper, below the mantle of Seattle's soccer history and closer to its core.

For John Best, the experience was something like love at first sight.

It was the spring of 1974, the dawn of the first iteration of the Sounders in the original North American Soccer League. Best was in Seattle to interview with Herman Sarkowsky, a local businessman with a stake in the expansion team, about becoming its first head coach. Sitting at the front desk of Sarkowsky's office that morning was a young woman named Claudia Goldsmith, who was smitten by Best's handsome looks and soccer-player physique. She was also slightly mortified to be wearing the purple pantsuit she broke out only when running behind on laundry.

Charmed by their small talk before Best was called into her boss's office and fearing she had missed her chance, she implored a coworker who was set to show the job candidate around town to bring him by the J&M Café, which she often frequented with her friends. Best walked into the dimly lit Pioneer Square bar later that evening having nailed his interview, he and Goldsmith spent the whole night talking, and they moved in together a few weeks later.

Claudia found out years later that Best had actually asked her coworker where that "nice young woman" from the front desk might be hanging out that night, that he hadn't required any prodding to get pointed in her direction, and the couple held onto the anecdote as a private inside joke from there on out.

"John was thinking that he did it, and I was thinking that I did it," Claudia said. "But we both wanted to see each other. He also fell in love with Seattle. Of course, with me, but also Seattle."

The Emerald City in the early 1970s was a backwater in more ways than one. Still decades away from the grunge craze of the '90s, and with the 1962 World's Fair that precipitated the building of the Space Needle having failed to establish the global respect city leaders craved, Seattle possessed a not-insignificant inferiority complex. That it was so isolated from the rest of the country, both geographically and in national recognition, only exacerbated that feeling.

If you're picturing gray skies and remote logging roads between towering evergreen trees, that's a slight exaggeration, but it isn't that far off.

Prior to the Sounders' arrival in 1974, the SuperSonics were the only professional game in town — and the NASL and NBA of the era were both dwarfed primarily by baseball but also the National Football League. The Sounders themselves were actually part of a gambit to attract the more prestigious NFL. Lamar Hunt, the owner of the Kansas City Chiefs and a member of that league's expansion committee, also owned the NASL's Dallas Tornado, and he persuaded Sarkowsky, Lloyd Nordstrom and the rest of Seattle's power brokers to shoot for a soccer franchise first.

The region's soccer scene was not exactly thriving at the time. The sport had roots in the Puget Sound dating back to the 1800s. But as in other major American cities of the era, it was considered an immigrant pastime played mostly by pockets of newcomers: in Seattle, that meant the Norwegians, Germans, English and Irish. The game was divorced from the mainstream. At the dawn of the 1970s, fewer than 8,000 boys were registered as players by the state's youth soccer association.

For most, that lack of ground-level support would have been a drawback; for Best, it tapped into his entrepreneurial instincts.

Best was born in Liverpool, a gritty industrial city in England's northwest. He began his career under legendary Liverpool FC coach Bill Shankly, who would go on to lead the Reds to three league titles, two FA Cups and a European championship. Best's own career path was more modest, at least until he moved abroad. Prior to his retirement and subsequent hiring by the Sounders, he was a five-time NASL all-star with Hunt's Dallas Tornado.

Best viewed the United States as the land of opportunity. It had resurrected his career, lifted him out of a life of who knows what in Liverpool, delivered him to Claudia. He approached growing the sport he loved in his adopted country with a missionary's zeal — his way of repaying America for all it had given to him. So while many would have been irked by Seattle's soccer ignorance, its first professional coach was more patient.

. Those impulses shaped Best's team selection. A defender during his playing days, Best might have been expected to build the team out of the back. Instead, knowing first-time fans were unlikely to appreciate the nuances of a tactical and disciplined 0–0 draw, and though his team could play lock-down defense when necessary, the Englishman was careful to stock his roster with plenty of capable attackers as well.

"He knew that even at the expense of losing games, he had to access the most offensive side of the game for the new crowd," explained Goldsmith, later a Best herself, to whom John was eager to impart his expertise during their courtship. "He knew what he had to put on the field, even if it wasn't the same team he would have put on the field if they had a fan base that only wanted them to win."

If there was only one shot to make a favorable first impression, and much like their successors did more than four decades later, Best's Sounders nailed it. In front of a capacity crowd at Memorial Stadium in the city center, Willie Penman opened the scoring of their inaugural match with a long-range strike less than two minutes in, leading the way to a 4–0 Seattle rout of Denver on May 12, 1974.

The Sounders played in front of six sellout crowds during that first season, missing the playoffs but compiling a respectable 13-7 record, and reached the NASL quarterfinals a year later. Legend has it that it never rained during a home game at Memorial during those first two seasons, helping to drive up crowds — "I think we got some assistance from above," Best once said.

Off the field, too, Best's outgoing personality had a favorable impact.

"We made him basically the face of the franchise," said Jack Daley, the club's first general manager. "He was a great public speaker. He was a good-looking guy. He almost had a Pied Piper personality. I can't recall anybody who John Best ever met in Seattle that was turned off by him."

And perhaps more crucial than anything else, Best actively recruited players who shared his passion for growing the sport from the ground up. Stories of the camps he and his charges hosted during those early years are legion. No request was too small, no northwestern town too remote to caravan out to for player appearances.

Frank MacDonald, a senior at Centralia High located two hours down Interstate 5, reached out to the team about hosting a clinic in his hometown a few weeks after the Sounders reached the 1977 Soccer Bowl. When an awestruck MacDonald walked out of the front of the high school to meet the traveling delegation, he was stunned to see that the Sounders hadn't just sent down a few reps, they'd sent down four of their very best players, including captain Adrian Webster.

His burgeoning affection for the game validated by the experience, MacDonald would later work for the Sounders' PR team himself and become one of Cascadia's leading soccer historians.

"For me, it was one of those boyhood experiences, even though I was 17," MacDonald said, "that confirmed everything I'd heard about that team, that they were involved in the community, how approachable they were. It solidified everything for me."

Before Pam Copple was the president of the Washington Youth Soccer Association, she was a single mother trying to wrap her head around the sport her daughter picked up one day at school. Her age group was in desperate need of coaches, and Copple volunteered despite knowing little about the game. In over her head, Copple reached out to the Sounders, and to her pleasant surprise, the club promised to send out a couple of players to her next practice for guidance.

"The Sounders were real open [to helping me] if I called: 'I don't know what I'm doing, I need a clinic,'" Copple said. "The Sounders were always there to support me and the kids that I was working with. And I was there to support them."

Those personal touches might not seem like much, drops in the proverbial bucket. But taken together, all those connections added up. A young man named Adrian Hanauer fell in love with the game under the artificial lights of the Kingdome, a passion that would lead to him buying a troubled minor-league soccer club later on down the line. Schmetzer was just one of a generation of local coaches to have gotten his start either playing for the NASL Sounders or daydreaming about it in their backyards. They were the ones whose efforts kept the sport alive after that league went bust in the '80s.

Copple would go on to spearhead the valiant but unsuccessful bid to host 1994 World Cup games at Husky Stadium, and under her leadership player participation under the WYSA umbrella ballooned. Numbers had been trending upward ever since the Sounders arrived in town, from 8,000 to more than 77,000 registered players by the time the NASL folded. And it wasn't just the region's little boys who were inspired — girls, in the years after Title IX was passed, started to envision a future in which they could play professionally too.

Michelle Akers, considered one of the greatest female soccer players ever and the first superstar of the U.S. women's national team, grew up in the Seattle suburb of Shoreline. A not-insignificant chunk of the inaugural 1991 Women's World Cup champions were blooded in the region's highly competitive semi-pro leagues. Hope Solo grew up in Central Washington and attended UW under Lesle Gallimore, another influential pioneer. On the men's side, longtime U.S. national team midfielder and future sporting director Chris Henderson carved out a path that fellow locals like DeAndre Yedlin and Jordan Morris would later follow.

What made Seattle such a good soccer town? Modern-day management certainly played a role, but they were building upon a grassroots movement that had been carefully cultivated for decades.

THREE

As THE SUN SET behind Arizona's Catalina Foothills, Sigi
Schmid soaked in the view from the patio of the team hotel
and sighed contentedly. The Sounders were midway through
preseason camp in February of 2016, their base in Tucson a
welcome reprieve from the rainy gloom back home. Schmid
discussed tactics and roster building, but he was most eloquent
when widening the scope. He was in a contemplative mood.

Though his best-laid plans would be trashed in just a few
weeks' time, if he sensed the coming doom, he didn't show it.
For now, the 62-year-old coach felt rejuvenated, as alive as he
had in years.

Schmid suffered a health scare the previous September that
could have ended his career. Few outside Schmid's tight inner
circle knew the specifics, only that it was heart related, that he
was hospitalized for four days and that he was forced to take in
a Sounders home match from a hospital bed. The scare was serious enough that Schmid polled his wife, Valerie, and their four
children on whether or not he should call it quits. Assured by
the doctor that there was no inordinate risk if he were to return
to the sidelines, the verdict was unanimous.

There was another reason behind the five votes of confidence: "Everybody knows I'd probably be a miserable guy to be around if I wasn't coaching," Schmid said. All told, he missed only a pair of games while regaining his strength, but even that layoff had a profound effect.

"I hate missing games," Schmid said. "I love the fact that my kids are all married, but I had to miss a couple games [for their weddings] for that to happen. So last year, going through what I did, it just reinforced to me that this is what I love to do. I want to do it for as long as I can and as long as people think I'm capable of doing it."

Schmid paused, raising his eyes to a desert sky painted with streaks of indigo and orange by the setting sun. The last season had ended in disappointment, and Sounders fans were restless. Yet he was inspired more than cowed by the challenges ahead — first and foremost fitting incoming star rookie and homegrown golden boy Jordan Morris into an already crowded front line. As he drew imaginary formations and movements on the table in front of him with animated hands, you could almost see his vision brought forth into life.

"It's still what drives me," Schmid said. "I'm still excited about it every day."

As always with Schmid, though, there was touchiness under the surface. He had struggled with his weight since he was young. He'd dealt with snide comments about his wide-bodied figure, both imagined and real, and over the years, he'd come to carry his excess pounds almost out of defiance. The question about whether that weight could have contributed to his heart issue might have been an obvious one, but the coach scowled, furrowed his brow and dismissed the notion with vehemence. It was a hereditary condition, he explained, nothing that any amount of exercise or dieting would've done much to prevent.

"When I decide I want to lose weight, I lose weight," Schmid said. "Part of the reason for me having not lost weight early in my career was really a stubbornness within me. Somehow there was a perception I got from some people that all of a sudden you're going to become a smarter coach if you lose weight. I thought that was such a stupid thing."

Part of him wondered if he had risen as high as he might have had he lost that weight, or if those perceptions stunted his potential. He had succeeded at every level, from college to the pros, lifting NCAA national championship trophies as well as MLS Cups. Unlike contemporaries Bruce Arena and Bob Bradley, though, two men who charted similar career paths, Schmid never got a shot to head up the U.S. national team.

"It was a perception that was maintained," Schmid said, still hung up on the question about his weight. "I'm not going to say which organization, or at what level, but it's sort of there. I'm sure I could probably sue if I wanted to."

Schmid racked up more than 250 MLS wins, more than any other coach at that stage in the league's history, but critics were quick to dismiss most of those as *regular-season* wins and point to Arena's five league titles to Schmid's two.

So even if Schmid was refreshed and pensive at the dawn of the 2016 season, there was an underlying self-consciousness too. To get a fuller sense of why, it was necessary to rewind the decades to his childhood, back to a bicultural upbringing that had him straddling two worlds from the start.

Siegfried Schmid was born on March 20, 1953, in Tübingen, West Germany, into an evocative time and place. He didn't stay long, moving with his parents to Southern California when he was three, but even in absentia he always maintained a link to his homeland.

The cultural influences within the Schmid household remained strong: his mother, Doris, was such a renowned cook of German food that she often headed up group meals at the local

German-American social club, of which his father, Fritz, was a proud member. The family's diet was so European that despite coming of age in Los Angeles, Schmid claimed not to have tried his first taco or eaten his first shrimp until his late teens.

It went beyond cuisine. Schmid spent his adolescent summers in Tübingen visiting extended family, keeping one foot in the Old World. He describes this biculturalism mostly in positive terms, but with World War II still so close in the rearview mirror, others didn't always see it that way.

"There was a point where I got called names because I was German," Schmid said. "You got called Nazi and stuff like that. You would start to wonder, 'Why is that?'"

Since his parents spoke German at home, Schmid began school without much of a grasp on English, and as a teenager he developed a stutter that intensified whenever he was asked to speak in front of groups.

Soccer, playing the role sports so often do for ill-at-ease teens, served as an outlet. Doris, too, was an important figure, his emotional support system and the one with whom he shared his soft side. Her death when Sigi was 23 also left an indelible mark. Many years later, during his induction into the National Soccer Hall of Fame, his sadness that she couldn't be there for such a professional triumph still choked him up and brought him to tears.

His relationship with Fritz was more complicated. Once, in high school, father refused to allow son to attend a Friday night football game, just because. His explanation was simple, if maddening to Sigi: "Because you need to learn what 'no' means."

Fritz had been a German prisoner of war in World War II. He was captured soon after the Battle of Normandy and spent the remainder of the war working as a farmhand in England. The experience could have hardened Fritz, left him bitter and mean. Instead, the English farmer he worked for treated him with remarkable kindness, given the circumstances. The two men actually exchanged annual Christmas and Easter cards for years afterward.

Fritz did not offer those details freely to his son.

"It's something he holds within himself," Sigi said. "I have to pry that out of him."

Schmid held things similarly close to his chest. To those who didn't know him well — and even to some of his players — he could seem distant and aloof. It was only over time that one came to appreciate his dry sense of humor and his fierce loyalty to the subset of players he knew he could depend on.

Schmid eventually came to appreciate the discipline and work ethic his father helped instill, as frustrating as his methods were at the time. Fritz played a pivotal role in his career choices as well. Sigi originally wanted to major in English; Fritz didn't see much of a future in writing (or coaching, for that matter) and strongly encouraged him toward something more practical.

Later, that accounting degree would come in handy.

One afternoon in the summer of 1980, a trio of UCLA upper-classmen waltzed into the bare-bones office of their first-year head coach with unwelcome news. The Bruins had struggled the season prior, and with an inexperienced leader at the helm, the three of them didn't feel all that optimistic about the upcoming campaign either. Maybe they ought to just take a redshirt and see where things stood in '81.

Schmid knew he didn't have much leverage, so he offered his players a deal. If they gave him the first three games and the squad struggled early, they could sit out the rest of the season with no hard feelings. The Bruins started 3-0, and everything else snowballed from there.

"You know that if we had walked, it could have derailed your career before it even started," one of those players, Charles

Fisher, liked reminding Schmid whenever they crossed paths further down the road.

Though Schmid kept this from his players at the time, he harbored similar doubts. Such was the tenuous state of U.S. soccer in the 1980s. At the beginning of the decade, the heady days of the North American Soccer League had given way to an irreversible decline. Within a few years the league had folded, and the sport plummeted into a period of darkness. Every player and coach of a certain age was forced to ask himself a tough question: *Do I really want to go into something that's dying?*

Schmid hedged his bets. For six years after earning his MBA, he worked full time as a practicing accountant while coaching whenever he found spare time. Even after UCLA offered him a full-time gig, it required swallowing a 40 percent pay cut, and Schmid still kept books for his friends on the side to keep that door cracked. The fresh-faced coach made a promise to himself: win a national title within three years or give up the dream and go back to accounting for good. It took five seasons, but his Bruins showed enough promise to keep him engaged.

Schmid's teams won national championships in 1985, 1990 and 1997. He quickly established himself as one of the leading coaches of the era, alongside Arena at the University of Virginia and Bradley at Princeton. Their personal battles helped all of them hone their respective crafts, even if they wouldn't have admitted as much at the time. They also helped form the bedrock of American soccer coaching philosophy for a generation.

The feud between Schmid and Arena was especially fierce. Arena, more often than not, got the better of his West Coast rival, first at the collegiate level and then in the pros. Arena's Galaxy knocked Schmid's Sounders out of the MLS playoffs in three of their first six seasons, with Seattle not winning a series against L.A. until year seven.

Schmid described their dynamic by way of a story about a

long-ago dinner with longtime NC State coach George Taran-tini, one he told in vivid detail during that aforementioned Hall of Fame speech.

"Sigi, I have to tell you this," Tarantini told him — Schmid mimicking the Greek-American's thick accent and pretending to hold a cigarette between his fingers. "I know you and Bruce are very competitive. And I know every time Bruce's team wins a national championship, you slit your wrists just a little. But Sigi, I tell you, every time a UCLA player plays for the national team, Bruce, he slits his wrists just a little.'"

Over the years, ill will turned to mutual respect. By the 2010s, Schmid and Arena could appear downright chummy on the sidelines. Each settled gracefully into his role as the game's accomplished, aging figurehead.

There was but a single, glaring difference between their career paths. Arena got to fulfill his ultimate career ambition not just once but twice, coaching the U.S. men's national team (USMNT) from 1998 to 2006 and again getting the nod after Jurgen Klinsmann was fired in late 2016. Schmid, meanwhile, never even got an interview. Occasionally, he allowed himself to pout. Mostly, he contented himself with trying to become the best MLS coach he could be, even after it became clear that the job he wanted above all others would never be his.

Schmid was a meticulous and prolific notetaker. Even deep within the digital age, when most had long since switched over to Microsoft Word, Schmid still preferred to write notes out by hand. He even used the same type of yellow graph paper he'd been jotting on since his UCLA days, a holdover from his time as an accountant.

"Whenever he sees a new notebook, he gets all jazzed up," said his son, Kurt, a Sounders scout who doubled as Schmid's personal tech guy. "Like most guys his age, he's not the most computer literate."

Schmid's app of choice was old-school solitaire, which he could play for hours at a time while he decompressed. Once, after a program update, his beloved, outdated game was accidentally deleted. ("Immediately," Kurt said, "I got a phone call.")

Schmid took notes during meetings and rewrote them directly afterward for clarity. He recorded pre- and postseason sit-downs with players and coaches alike, brainstormed tactics, filled out lineups both real and hypothetical. Deep inside his home office existed never-used formations for Bruins squads long forgotten by everybody except former players and a head coach with a famously long memory.

That yellow graph paper got plenty of use during the first few months of 2016. Seattle's first-choice XI was edited and re-edited, written by hand in permanent ink but consistently changing.

First, the Sounders completed their prolonged courtship of Morris, the son of the club's team physician who had blown up into one of the hottest young prospects in American soccer during his two and a half years at Stanford. As Seattle had fended off multiple European suitors for Morris's signature, including Werder Bremen of the German Bundesliga, his addition was a genuine public relations coup.

On paper, though, it was more of an awkward fit. Seattle's two best and highest-paid players, forwards Clint Dempsey and Obafemi Martins, already occupied Morris's natural position. The team had in fact been built around the chemistry of that attacking pair, and it had also picked up Paraguayan international Nelson Valdez as an additional reinforcement the previous summer. Schmid seemed undaunted.

"You can never have too many good players," Schmid said at Morris's introductory press conference, articulating the closest thing he had to an overarching coaching philosophy.

Soccer pundits like to group coaches under two distinct labels: the ideologists and the pragmatists, those who stick rigidly to their preferred playing style and those whose tactics are more fungible depending on how badly they need a given result. Think Pep Guardiola's famous possession-heavy FC Barcelona teams versus Jose Mourinho's chameleon-like Chelsea squads.

That categorization isn't as cut and dried as some like to pretend — even the most dogmatic sometimes need to adjust, and every coach has at least some idea of how he would like to play. But if there were such a spectrum, Schmid definitely edged closer to pragmatic. If some coaches started with the system and plugged in pieces from there, Schmid started with his star players and catered his style of play to their strengths.

Few things stuck in the craw of Schmid and those close to him more than the perception that the old coach was somehow rigid or stuck in his ways. If anything, tactically, at least, he could swing too far the other way, tinkering and adapting so often that players sometimes wanted for clearer-cut roles.

Throughout the successes of 2014, when Seattle won both the Supporters' Shield as regular-season champions and the U.S. Open Cup, Schmid stuck mostly to a two-forward deployment that allowed Dempsey and Martins to work off one another up front. His strategy wasn't particularly complex — basically, play steady defense at the back and let Deuce and Oba make magic happen every so often — but it worked.

The problems began the following season, when Martins got injured and Dempsey suspended. Ahead of the new year, then, nothing was set in stone. Schmid was compelled to experiment. With Morris in the fold, Schmid concocted a 4-3-3 formation to cram as many of his talented forwards onto the field as possible. Morris, Dempsey, Martins and Valdez would all shuffle through the front line, with one of them sitting out each weekend to rest.

That would save the veterans' legs for the stretch run, the coach explained, as well as allow him to slowly integrate the rookie into the team. If Schmid saw the holes in this strategy — how the attack might struggle to build chemistry with so many constantly shifting parts, or whether prideful superstars like Dempsey would willingly accept lesser roles — he glossed over them.

That February evening in Tucson, Schmid was ebullient.

He'd spent part of the off-season in Italy studying the training methods of AS Roma. This was a habit he'd gotten into at UCLA, biannual trips abroad to pick colleagues' brains — he once spent a memorable winter observing then-Stuttgart and future German national team coach Joachim Low — but one he hadn't practiced in years.

He forgot how invigorating it could be. Observing others always forced him to get more introspective about his own methods, and he came away newly aware of what had long been a core principle of his coaching: adapt or die.

"You have to thirst for knowledge every day," Schmid told me. "The day you stop doing that is the day you stagnate and go backwards as a coach. Everything is cyclical in life. That's one of the beliefs I have. Even you in your job, I'm sure there are days where it's really cool and other days where it can be a drag. When you expand that, there are probably months where it feels like a drag and months where it seems very exciting. So you go through this wave. It's the same thing for coaches.

"You go through these waves of games and it's really good and you're on the edge. And you sort of — not necessarily become complacent — but you sort of start to flow along. Sometimes it's because you become distracted and focus on other things. But that's human nature. At the end of the day, you come back to your team.

"Those valleys of stagnation or lesser motivation aren't very long. You have more peaks where you're really trying to get into it and get things going. I think everybody goes through valleys."

That evening, in retrospect, was a peak. The drop to the valley on the other side was steep.

Less than a fortnight before the new season, Martins turned in his transfer request. Though the Sounders could have technically held him to his contract, they couldn't come close to matching the annual wages on offer in China. Instead of risking team chemistry by retaining what would have been a very unhappy player, they let Martins walk.

The season got off to a wholly dispiriting start. A scheduling quirk meant the quarterfinals of the CONCACAF Champions League took place before MLS action kicked off, and Seattle was swiftly dispatched by Mexican powerhouse Club America, 5–3 over two legs.

League play could hardly have started more disastrously. Second-year defender Oniel Fisher was red-carded for trying to scissor-kick a Kansas City opponent's legs, and the Sounders lost the home opener 1–0 to Sporting. They lost the second game, too, after backup goalkeeper Tyler Miller whiffed on a late attempted clearance in Salt Lake City, and the third to rival Vancouver again on home turf.

Instead of being eased in, Morris was tossed into the deep end in the wake of Martins's departure. It was both a blessing and a curse that the young forward wore his emotions on his sleeve — a blessing because it made him easy to root for, fans easily identifying with his breakthroughs; a curse because when things weren't going well, Morris looked like the saddest young man in the entire world.

The rookie was held scoreless in his first three MLS matches, a drought that would extend well into the second month of the season. The scowl on his face deepened and his shoulders drooped a little further with each passing match. At 0-3-0, his body language spoke for the whole team.

The journey to the breaking point began with the break.

Seattle steadied itself somewhat with a hard-fought 1–0 win

over Montreal on April 2 and a 1–1 draw in Houston one week later. Still, though, the team hadn't played well. They hadn't adjusted to the new formation, and Schmid was so desperate that he pulled Morris from the starting lineup prior to the Impact game.

The coach racked his brain for a potential solution. One morning at his condo in downtown Bellevue, preparing to leave for work, Schmid was so fully immersed in his thoughts that he missed the first step off his back porch, slipping and landing with a heavy thud.

Initially, he held out hope that he'd just badly twisted his ankle, but X-rays showed a broken left fibula. For more than a month, he hobbled around the training facility on crutches, often taking in practices from the back of a cart parked off the near sideline.

Proximity had long been key to Schmid's success: "I really think my strength as a coach is being close to the team," he said. "My strength as a coach is being a bug in your ear, in a good way."

Proximity was also a major reason why he and Hanauer worked so well together for so many years. The two men first met in the early 2000s, when Hanauer's Sounders partnered with Schmid's Galaxy as a loose minor-league affiliate. They kept in touch through the years — controversially so for a few weeks in late 2008, when the Crew accused expansion Seattle of tampering while Schmid was still under contract with Columbus.

During those heady first few years in the Emerald City, when attendance grew steadily upward with each passing season and every trophy was treated more like a pleasant surprise than a birthright, the line of communication between coach and owner was remarkably open. Hanauer was honest about the fact that although he knew the game on some level, he was no soccer expert. Schmid was more than happy to fill in the blanks. The owner would often dial his coach on his commute home from the office just to check in.

After Hanauer ceded the general manager role to Lagerwey to concentrate on the business side, though, distance started to expand between him and Schmid. Those phone calls were less frequent, then nearly nonexistent. Once omnipresent on the sidelines at Sounders practices, Hanauer now went weeks without appearing.

In a similar way, Schmid began to sense his influence over his players waning, too, after he broke his leg. Unable to easily move around, he delegated more and more tasks to his assistants. The changing vibe wasn't immediately obvious. In the weeks following Schmid's tumble, the Sounders went 3-1-0, with Morris scoring in all four games after finally breaking through against Philadelphia.

Once the false peak gave way to another valley, though, the shifting dynamic began to show itself. After another two-match losing streak, the trip to the East Coast in late May and early June contributed to the strain. With tempers flaring and the team continuing to struggle, the last thing the team needed was a week cramped together in close quarters.

Aaron Kovar's goal in New England could have represented a turning point.

In the seventh minute at Gillette Stadium, Kovar gathered a bouncing ball with his preferred left foot, looped it over a defender's head like a crossover and smashed it into the net with his right. The third-year midfielder had been one of the rare pleasant surprises of the young season, and his improvement seemed to have been crystalized by that moment of pure skill.

The lead stood for less than 15 minutes.

In a freakish bit of bad luck, Zach Scott's attempted clearance smashed into Erik Friberg's foolishly outstretched arm — a handball that turned into a converted penalty kick. Another setback: Evans took a cross to the face in the 40th minute and had to be taken off to undergo concussion protocol. The final blow came 11 minutes from time, with a long-range Revs strike that skipped off the spongy turf and beneath a sprawling Stefan Frei in goal.

Spirits were low enough already before the team arrived for the flight to Washington, D.C., at Logan Airport, where some players spotted Schmid and Lagerwey engaged in a heated conversation at one of the terminal's restaurants. The coach and GM sat across from one another, their hand gestures and body language suggesting that some long-simmering tempers were finally coming to the fore. Even if they couldn't make out the exact words of the exchange, the optics were not helpful for a group as bereft of self-confidence as it was.

"What's going to happen now? Am I going to be traded? I'm for sure gone,'" Evans said. "Every guy is thinking that in the back of their minds. Some guys are also thinking, 'This sucks. We're shit right now.' You can't have that. It just puts all these images in the back of people's heads that shouldn't be there."

There was a trickle-down effect throughout the traveling party. The assistant coaches were angry at themselves and assumed the players were mad at them too; the players thought the feeling of frustration went the other way and kept a wide berth. Where a well-timed joke might have helped ease tensions and bridge the divide, instead they kept to themselves and stewed.

"OK, I get it, we're professionals," Evans said. "We get paid to play the game. We should enjoy every minute of it, because we're making hundreds of thousands of dollars. That's just not how it is. That is the wrong perception. Every day, guys come in and worry about their job. 'Am I going to get traded today?' No matter what anybody tells you, that's what they think about — all of the time.

"When we're winning, everything's great. The media is on your side, everybody is happy. Once we lose, nobody even comes around and shakes hands in the locker room. People think it's one big happy thing, but when we lose a game, they're pissed at us and we're pissed at ourselves."

In American sports, stability is accepted as an inherent virtue. Our coaching legends include Bear Bryant, who led the University of Alabama's football program for nearly three decades, and Mike Krzyzewski, whose reign as Duke's basketball coach stood at 37 years as of writing. The window tends to be slightly tighter at the pro level, but not entirely: both Chuck Noll, who coached the Pittsburgh Steelers during parts of four decades, and Red Auerbach, who was an active part of the Boston Celtics for more than half a century, are lionized. Longevity is looked upon as a success in and of itself.

In European soccer, with the glaring exception of Sir Alex Ferguson's long reign at Manchester United, that premise was often questioned. To get too comfortable was to stagnate. An infusion of fresh blood was often necessary to reach loftier heights.

British journalist Jonathan Wilson cited a three-year rule he attributed to legendary Hungarian coach Bela Guttmann. At the top level of the game, the idea goes, three years was the maximum life span for successful teams. That time frame could be stretched a bit when applied to MLS, where the pressure was less acute than it is in the biggest European leagues. It wasn't always cut and dry; with heavy roster turnover or a shift in tactical emphasis, the rule could be staved off.

The overall logic, though, rang true. Even the very best coaches struggled to prevent their players from eventually tuning them out. Messages got stale over time.

When the team landed in Washington, D.C., and arrived at the hotel, Schmid called for an impromptu team meeting. Usually so attuned to the rhythms of his players, this time the old coach misread the room.

On their one night off in the nation's capital, with a precious chance to blow off some steam, the last thing the players wanted was another lecture. In front of a room full of grumpy faces, Schmid launched into a familiar parable about a former player of his at UCLA who wasn't the most gifted but had an extraordinary work ethic and willed himself to a lengthy and successful career.

The message wasn't *inaccurate*, per se — with multiple stars injured or away on international duty, the group sitting before him really did need to band together and become greater than the sum of its parts in order to win games. But after seven years, at least among some of the veterans, Schmid's words fell on deaf ears.

Immediately afterward, Evans called his agent: "I'm done here. I can't do this anymore," Evans told him, asking him to put out feelers for potential trade destinations.

"It had been too long and things were starting to hit the fan for me personally. I felt like I needed something new at the time. I had to get out of this situation to give me peace of mind."

At the midway point of a season in the throes of a death spiral, at least at that point in time, Evans wasn't alone in that sentiment.

FOUR

Osvaldo Alonso skulked around the Walmart sporting goods department, waiting for the security guard to turn his back to make his move.

This was in the summer of 2007, when he was still an upstanding member of the Cuban national soccer team, which was in the United States for that year's Gold Cup. Though he knew before he left the island that June that he planned on defecting and never coming back, he told no one — not his parents, not his younger siblings, not his friends.

"You had to keep quiet," Alonso said. "You never knew who was next to you. I never said anything about that. Just make your own decision and do it."

This wasn't his first trip abroad with the national team, so he had a feel for the patterns. Security details for tournaments in South America or elsewhere in the Caribbean were comparatively loose, but in the United States, players weren't even allowed to walk down to the hotel lobby to grab a candy bar without a chaperone for fear of defection.

Alonso realized his best shot to sneak away was at a team dinner or shopping excursion, but through the first two games, he hadn't found a suitable opening. Ahead of the group-stage finale against Honduras, with Cuba about to go three-and-out, he felt time slipping away. The visit to the Houston-area Walmart was his best, last chance.

The guards tried to keep the teammates corralled in certain sections of the store, but they were no match for the group's collective exuberance. The sons of communism dove into their fleeting brush with capitalism with abandon, filling shopping carts with cleats, underwear and souvenirs for loved ones back home.

Amid the chaos, Alonso found himself suddenly alone. Head bowed, he didn't hesitate, walking out the mechanical sliding doors and into a blinding Texas sun. For five excruciatingly long minutes, he strode with his head down without pausing before he finally swiveled for a glimpse over his shoulder to see if he was being followed.

"Before that, it was all about looking forward," Alonso said. "*Go, go, go, go.* If somebody saw me, I don't know what I would have done — I probably would have ran. I just looked forward."

Momentarily free, Alonso felt anxiety creeping outward from his core. Having so carefully waited for his moment, he had hardly allowed himself to imagine what it would be like once he wiggled through the escape hatch. Frantic, Alonso asked passing strangers if they spoke Spanish and if, more vitally, they had a cell phone he might borrow for a quick minute.

He never caught his Good Samaritan's name. Years later, the man somehow tracked down Alonso's phone number, having seen him on TV playing for the Sounders and wanting to relay how proud he was. But in the moment, everything was a blur. The stranger allowed Alonso to call his friends in Miami and even gave him a ride to the bus station.

It wasn't until the Greyhound pulled out of its dock that Alonso finally exhaled. On that 18-hour bus ride from Houston to Miami, alone with his thoughts and without so much as a magazine as a distraction, he began to ponder all he'd left behind as well as what he stood to gain.

Alonso's origin story was on the extreme end of the spectrum, to be sure. But it hit on themes common not just around Major League Soccer but within the confines of the Sounders locker room.

MLS has been by far the most diverse of the top professional sports leagues in the United States. At the beginning of the 2016 season, 67 countries from five continents were represented on MLS rosters. As of the most recent Elias Sports Bureau study in 2015, 43 percent of the league's players hailed from outside of the United States and Canada, dwarfing second-place Major League Baseball (26.5 percent), the National Hockey League (26.4 percent), the NBA (20 percent) and especially the NFL (2.8 percent).

The 2016 Sounders roster was stocked with players from 13 different countries, including a Cuban defector in Alonso, a proud native of the tiny Caribbean island of St. Vincent in Oalex Anderson and Paraguayan international Nelson Valdez, who came from such modest means that he spent his two years as a professional functionally homeless.

Such diversity posed challenges, most obviously communication but also culture shock and the potential for teams to break into factions. But it also, at its best and as the Sounders would show by the end of the year, had the potential to meld all of these differences into a coherent whole better for all of the disparate backgrounds.

When Lamar Neagle was traded from Seattle to Montreal in 2012, he encountered an MLS expansion team struggling in its search of an identity. The Impact was plagued by everything from lack of organizational cohesion to amateurish facilities to the divide between minor-leaguers jumping up with the club and pricey incoming internationals.

Perhaps most damaging, especially on the field, was the lack of a lingua franca. During Montreal's first MLS season under American head coach Jesse Marsch, most of the training and game-planning sessions were conducted in English. There was a significant Italian influence, headed up by longtime Azzurri defender Alessandro Nesta, as well as the French-Canadian contingent native to Quebec.

On the first day of camp, both in the locker room and at team meals, players divided themselves into thirds based on their native tongues or mutual acquaintances. Neagle was just as guilty as anybody, sticking mostly with his American counterparts.

The impulse to gravitate toward one's own was understandable. The problem for Montreal was that as the season progressed, that never changed. You could almost draw a clean pie chart among the group dividing the cliques by English, Italian and French speakers. As Neagle put it: "Nobody ever switched lunch tables."

Bridging the cultural divide required effort and hard work. The Sounders, going all the way back to their inaugural season, have been better about that than most.

"There aren't as distinct lines," said Neagle, who would know, given that he's played for six professional clubs and the Sounders themselves during four different eras. "There are definitely groups, but not distinct lines."

Traditionally, the most obvious potential divide within the squad had been between the primarily English and primarily Spanish speakers, given Seattle's sizable Latino contingent from the outset that included Alonso, Colombian attacker Fredy Montero and Costa Rican defender Leo Gonzalez. California-born and fluent Spanish speaker Taylor Graham helped break down some of those walls by offering to translate during that first, formative preseason camp. The tone was set.

"There have always been guys that toe that line [between groups], and it's always easier to bring guys over through them," Neagle said.

Nearly a decade later, the Sounders boasted multiple players who could flit easily between social groups. Second-year midfielder Cristian Roldan, the son of El Salvadoran and Guatemalan immigrants, was comfortably bilingual, as was rookie defender Tony Alfaro, another California native. Star forward Dempsey, who grew up in Texas playing in a predominantly Mexican rec league, could also hold his own. Alonso had long since become fluent in English, and Valdez, who was fluent in four languages before he even arrived in Seattle in mid-2015, was a quick learner.

The end result was a locker room without clearly demarcated boundaries, and team chemistry benefitted.

That's not to say the Sounders were the closest team in the world. There were distinct pockets inside the locker room, and the same players tended to always leave the team facility together. The single youngsters would chatter away about that evening's plans while the married veterans kept mostly to themselves, in a rush to get home to their families.

Seattle teams tended to be more mature than most of their MLS counterparts. Goalkeeper Stefan Frei joked that every newcomer got engaged within a year of signing with the club, so adult was the general vibe. That could occasionally come as a detriment to team bonding. The Sounders didn't typically gather on bye weekends to grab beers and shoot pool.

What the squad had always done well relative to the rest of the league, however, was blur the lines that tended to form based on nationality or region. As the season threatened to shudder off the rails entirely, when they could have turned on one another in the face of adversity, that united front proved hugely important.

With the signing of Oalex Anderson to a first-team contract in March of 2016, another demographic group expanded its influence within the club.

Anderson's journey to the pros began on the island of St. Vincent, a tiny speck in the southeast corner of the Caribbean. Even when factoring in the outer-lying, even tinier specks known as the Grenadines, the population barely edged over 100,000. St. Vincent was remote, both its blessing and its curse. The island was beautiful and mostly unspoiled, with lush white sand on one coast and black on the other due to a long-ago volcanic eruption. Without much tourism, the country retained a unique culture, both sporting and otherwise.

"When we're walking, we walk slow," said Myron Samuel, a forward on Seattle's minor-league squad in describing his homeland, "but when we're running, we run fast."

An international airport was set to connect St. Vincent with the wider world starting in early 2017, but given how many delays had plagued its construction since the project broke ground in 2008, most of the locals said they would believe it when they saw it. Most of them also conceded that even if the airport and the potential influx of tourists irrevocably changed the island, it would ultimately be for the better.

Physically stunning, this was not an easy place to come of age. There weren't many steady jobs, and many Vincentians grew up aimless, with uncertain futures. Others dreamed of a way out.

Anderson's trip off the island, not unlike the airport that eventually hoped to service it, came only after a series of false starts. Spotted by a Sounders scout at a holiday tournament in his home village one Christmas morning, Anderson broke his leg later the next year and lost his chance for a scholarship to Seattle University. The Sounders came calling again but offered only a minor-league deal. The lithe, explosive young forward again faced a roundabout route toward his ultimate goal.

Anderson finally signed the contract he'd long striven for following a standout performance at preseason camp in early 2016. He found a number of fellow island boys already on the roster — talented left back Joevin Jones out of Trinidad and Tobago, and defenders Oniel Fisher and Damion Lowe from Jamaica. Add to that representatives from places as far flung as Martinique, Haiti and Antigua on S2, the minor-league team, and the Sounders organization was as Caribbean influenced as any in MLS.

Though most of them originated from different countries, the island contingent clung tightly to one another. They were regulars at restaurants like Taste of the Caribbean in the Central District, where it smelled of slow-roasted jerk chicken and where Fisher's signed, framed jersey hung proudly next to posters of Usain Bolt and Bob Marley.

Culture was part of it. A shared realization of just how lucky they were to have the opportunity was too. It might not have seemed like much to outsiders, with most of them on the fringe of a roster in a league still fighting for relevance of its own, but to a bunch of guys who had grown up modestly, they were very much living their dreams.

Most of them had Ezra Hendrickson to thank. A St. Vincent native himself whose family moved to the United States when he was 13, the head coach of S2 was the patron saint of long-shot hopefuls from the islands.

"I want to help as many of the kids there as I can," said Hendrickson, who doubled as a Sounders assistant. "Because there are a lot of talented footballers, a lot of talented people. They just need an opportunity. Whatever I can do to ease that road or facilitate that transition, I'm willing to do. I think it's something I was put on Earth to do, to help."

Standing six foot three and still retaining the muscle of a central defender from his playing days, Hendrickson was easy to spot. For years, he'd been popping up at some obscure Caribbean scouting combine, or another. He's the one who found Anderson while at home for the holidays a few years ago. Hendrickson's dedication to the cause was admirable and went beyond base platitudes — who but a true believer would've showed up for a talent showcase hastily planned for his arrival *on Christmas morning?*

"If you grew up with our background, where we grew up and how we grew up, if you get this opportunity, you want to grasp it and make the most of it," Hendrickson said. "You don't want to let it slip through because you know, if you mess up, someone else will take it. All I need to do was get these guys' foot in the door. From there, their God-given talents, will and hunger are really going to propel them far."

Early on in the season, at least, Hendrickson's words seemed spot on. Anderson hadn't just made the roster; he quickly established himself as an impact sub. The 20-year-old winger was a raw, visceral thrill, his game best summarized by a single galloping run against Montreal in April. He split a pair of Impact defenders near midfield with a dribble straight out of a video game, sped into open space toward a stranded goalkeeper . . . and froze up in the penalty box, allowing his opponents enough time to backtrack and steal the ball.

Anderson wasn't quite there yet. The finishing touch still eluded him. But that moment in particular was a fleeting glimpse into exactly what Hendrickson saw on his scouting trips and why he spoke so passionately about his cause — the rare and special talent capable of propelling somebody to a better life.

Of course, not every immigrant story fit so neatly into established tropes. If stereotype demanded that immigrants to the United States arrive on these shores wracked with desperation, willing to risk it all and pay homage to an American Dream that often proved illusory, Sounders goalkeeper Stefan Frei offered a counterpoint.

For one, if it had been up to his 16-year-old self, Frei's family would never have left Switzerland. His soccer career was just taking off when they emigrated, and he was forced to watch from afar as his former Swiss teammates won the 2002 European U-17 Championship. For another, Frei could've become a U.S. citizen years ago but actively chose not to until finally beginning the naturalization process in late 2016.

Frei was first approached by the USMNT under former coach Bob Bradley toward the end of the 2000s. Headstrong and still in his early 20s at the time, Frei said thanks but no thanks. Even after a standout collegiate career at Cal Berkeley, he'd retained little affection for his new homeland. Some of that was personal: his parents divorced shortly after they arrived in the States, and his father — whose job was the sole reason they'd left in the first place — moved back to Switzerland. Watching his former teammates' Euro triumph didn't help Frei's mood.

"These guys were all getting big-time contracts, and I was at the local park trying to find a pickup game," Frei said.

Some of his reticence had to do with lifestyle and culture.

"At the time, the only place I had lived in was California," Frei said. "As much as I loved my time there, I got the sense of Americans as being very focused on their image, what they're driving, how much money they're making and that kind of deal. I didn't like that. I later realized that's a very California thing. I let it go through my head, and I still had it in the back of my mind that maybe I can go back to play for Switzerland at some point. I didn't want to lead [the United States] on."

Goalkeepers tended to be soccer's consistently best interviews. Something about the position seemed to draw the introspective types, and all of that time spent in isolation, on the lonely isle of your own penalty box, provided plenty of opportunity for deep thought.

Frei conformed with that stereotype, at least. He could riff at length on everything from European hip-hop to impressionist art to U.S. politics. He was characteristically thoughtful in discussing his left-leaning beliefs. A commitment to open borders and gay rights fit right in in liberal Seattle. It clashed, however, with the political movement that built to a crescendo throughout 2016.

Frei had emerged back on the U.S. national team radar the previous winter following a standout season with Seattle, and the pursuit only intensified as he carried that good form over into the new year. Even as the Sounders struggled, he was a lone bright spot in net, with strong hands and a cocksure self-possession.

For a little while, it appeared as though presidential candidate Donald Trump would undo the work of multiple eras of USMNT coaches who had attempted to persuade Frei to don red, white and blue. A country that would allow Trump to come to power was incompatible with his belief system, Frei reasoned. Ultimately, though, his desire to speak his mind — as well as the influence of like-minded Seattle friends — finally won out and inspired him to file his paperwork.

"There should be some meaning behind these things, citizenship and what you stand for," Frei said. "It's not just being opportunistic — 'oh, I can make some more cash; let's do it.' Also, speaking about politics, I don't want to speak about U.S. politics when I'm not American. I'm not going to start bashing someone that I have no right to bash. I'm waiting for that day, and when I start bashing, you'll know I have citizenship."

Nelson Valdez was a gifted storyteller — though his life story would've been compelling enough on its face even if he hadn't been. With movie star looks and as an emphatic user of hand gestures, Valdez could conjure up visions of dusty Paraguayan streets and add convincing layers of detail to the formative moments of his journey.

Like the period following the death of his cousin, when he was still 12 years old but already on the way to a drinking problem and his father caught him standing with a beer in hand with a group of local ne'er-do-wells.

"He only looked at me, but that look was such that I would have preferred him hitting me a thousand times," Valdez said. "It was as if he was saying, 'My son, you are lost and there is nothing else I can do for you.' That was the hardest blow I have ever had, and the blow that changed my life."

Or the time at the very beginning of his professional career when he spent two years functionally homeless, living under the bleachers at his club's stadium on a makeshift bed of cardboard; or how he used the very last of his savings to buy the one-way plane ticket to Germany for a mere tryout with Werder Bremen; or how during his first few months in Europe, he ate chicken and chips for every single meal because that was the only thing he knew how to order in broken German at local restaurants.

Valdez's various anecdotes were the stuff of the Most Interesting Man in the World advertising campaign.

He promised his mother, a diehard fan of the Paraguayan national team, that he would lead them to the World Cup one day — and scored the very goal that clinched qualification against Argentina in 2009. While playing for little Hercules in Spain's La Liga, he scored twice at the Camp Nou to topple Guardiola's mighty Barcelona.

He fought off would-be carjackers while playing for Borussia Dortmund in 2009, promising his wife he would never do anything so foolish again — then broke that pledge two years later, in Valencia, when the thieves actually did get away with the car but he managed to bust the back window with a well-placed rock.

"So I called the police and told them the car probably had a broken window, and with the description they found the car," Valdez said. "It turns out after they entered their home, they also found three or four firearms, so I was very lucky."

He once ran into a burning house to save his family's beloved dog and annually flew back home to personally deliver Christmas presents to nearly a thousand underprivileged kids who reminded him of who he once was.

This was a man who could do anything he put his mind to — except, it turned out, and to his increasing dismay, score goals in MLS. The man who felled Barca and fired his beloved country into the World Cup found himself stymied by the likes of the Columbus Crew and Colorado Rapids.

Valdez started and was held scoreless during Seattle's three-game season-opening losing streak, but it wasn't as though he was playing badly. He was putting himself in the right positions in front of net, and any striker will tell you that's half the battle. Keep doing that, and the goals will come. But they didn't. Valdez was blanked in April, lost most of May to a nagging calf injury and carried that goose egg into June and then July.

At $1.45 million per year, Valdez was Seattle's second-highest-paid player, and that number drew increasing criticism. Following a particularly listless performance in the 2–0 home loss to New York City FC, former Sounders forward Eddie Johnson went as far as to break typical decorum and rip a fellow player on social media.

"1.4 a year you gotta be special and create something on your own in a game like this they expected from me on 100k," Johnson wrote, referencing his own meager salary, taking a cheap shot Valdez couldn't really rebut while on that zero.

Some would've just cashed the checks and mailed it in; Valdez had never grown completely comfortable with that kind of money, and that wasn't his way regardless.

"I want to do well in Seattle and show the people why I'm here and who I am," Valdez said, practically beseechingly, around the season's halfway point. "I ask God that I don't get injured anymore and try to finish right here."

Pain etched in stark lines across his face, by midsummer Valdez was the Sounders as a whole personified. He was determined, however, to will himself out of his slump. He had come too far to succumb so easily to adversity. In that, he was not alone: nobody who had gone through what Alonso, Anderson and others like them had experienced was likely to roll over.

They all had too much on the line.

FIVE

BRAD EVANS WAS PART of a dying breed of American soccer players.

Though still in his early 30s, he was old enough to remember how far-fetched it'd felt that he'd be able to make a career out of this. When players of his generation were growing up, MLS still seemed like it could just as easily go bust as prosper. Even guys lucky enough to get on one of the league's rosters mostly made peanuts.

Soccer, truth be told, wasn't Evans's first love. His original passion was skateboarding, and his childhood bedroom on the outskirts of Phoenix doubled as a shrine to Tony Hawk.

Part of that was the state of the game in this country during his formative years. Fox Sports World launched in 1997, but its reach was limited, at least at first. Evans guessed that he didn't watch his first soccer match on TV until he was at least 14 years old and attended his first live professional match as a sophomore in college, when he scored free tickets to a Chivas USA game.

The sport was not in the Evans family's blood. They were a baseball tribe whose patriarch, Brad's grandfather, was a diehard Brooklyn then Los Angeles Dodgers fan. When soccer finally got its hooks into Brad during his early teens, his parents encouraged him and provided advice where they could, but the game was mostly alien to them.

Evans earned an athletic scholarship to UC Irvine but dared not dream much bigger than that until fate intervened. Schmid's son, Kyle, also played for the Anteaters, and so by happenstance spotted Evans during an especially strong performance and brought him aboard the U.S. U-20 team he coached.

The point is, soccer has always been more fungible to Evans than most. He still wasn't exactly sure what he would've otherwise done, career-wise — he was a social sciences major but wasn't always the most dedicated of students — only that he would've found a way to make it work somehow.

Even after Columbus drafted him in the second round of the 2007 SuperDraft, it took multiple interventions from his mother to prevent Evans from packing up his car, aiming it southwest and walking away from the game for good.

He'd injured his quad during that year's MLS Combine, hurt it again early in the season and was shut down for the season after four games. Across the country from his family and the long-distance girlfriend who would later become his wife, Evans was already in a funk before his roommate got cut three months in. Rookie contracts weren't guaranteed, and if he was spared the ax, all of a sudden his housing situation was thrown in flux too.

"Make your decision when you're healthy," his mom told him, time and time again, a phrase he repeated back to himself as a mantra during the darkest times.

One of the few bright spots: Evans bonded with second-year defender Chad Marshall, laying the seeds for a longtime friendship, finding company in their shared misery. Marshall was also out for the season after suffering a series of concussions that threatened to end his own career before it even started. With far too much free time on their respective hands, Evans helped Marshall remodel his new home in the Columbus suburbs — sanding and laying down hardwood floors, applying fresh coats of paint.

In return, Marshall offered Evans one of his spare rooms and gave him a break on rent. Even so, and despite living in one of the cheapest markets in MLS, Evans only barely made ends meet. Back then, the league minimum salary was $12,900, and he was near the bottom of the heap. His grandmother took to sending him — a *professional athlete*, remember — food cards so he could afford groceries.

"I was in the red," Evans said. Multiple times he had to ask his parents for help just to pay that month's bills.

A few years ago, when Marshall was cleaning out the house in preparation for a move across the country to unite with Evans in Seattle, he came across one of his former teammate's pay stubs buried in an old desk.

"After taxes, it was $400," Evans said. "And that was biweekly."

Coming out of such humble origins, MLS veterans typically skewed one way or the other. Some still seemed amazed by the fact they'd been able to scrape a living out of the game they loved. Others were less complacent. They still remembered the flush of shame of having to lean on extended family just to afford rent, the dark comedy in calling oneself a pro athlete while living below the federal poverty line. This group was determined to secure a more lucrative future for players like themselves further down the line.

Evans, secure in an identity less wrapped up in the game than most and with a keen awareness of his platform, belonged firmly in the latter camp.

Leadership didn't always come naturally to him. Skateboarding, after all, was more individualistic, and Evans liked that about it, the long hours of working in solitude for the payoff of even the simplest tricks.

As Evans got older, though, he noticed that people tended to follow his example. He had a brooding intensity to him, an energy others gravitated toward. At Irvine, he was named a cocaptain, a designation he's never taken lightly. The captaincy carries more weight to it in soccer than in any other sport, besides perhaps hockey. Captains are leaders inside the locker room first and foremost, but more than that, they're club ambassadors.

"I don't view the armband as a special power," said Evans, who became Seattle's captain in 2013. "I don't view it like I should play any better. What it represents to me is that it's somebody who's experienced, who's been around the block, who has relationships with referees and with other teams. I think there's a mutual respect between myself and other captains. You don't mind talking to the media, win, lose or draw, getting blown out or having a good game. It's not a superpower, but it's somebody who wants to represent the team in the right way, and the city, most importantly. That's what it's all about."

Sounders locker rooms tended to empty out quickly after losses. MLS rules mandated that teams open up the room to reporters no later than 15 minutes after the final whistle, but you'd be amazed by how quickly players can shower and change when faced with the prospect of standing in front of the camera after a painful defeat. Evans, though, almost without fail, waited around. He accepted it as part of his duty to speak for the team, no matter how disappointing the loss or how grating the questions may have been.

He was also, more so than most, willing to open up about topics outside the lines of a soccer field. That tendency could inspire blowback, like when he wrote on Twitter in response to then-presidential-candidate Donald Trump's infamous Cinco de Mayo taco bowl tweet that he would "play soccer for free if [he] could smash [Trump's] face in that bowl." Evans's sentiments went national, sucked into the highly polarized political vortex of the day, and that made some of the more corporate-minded folks around the club squeamish. He, though, never backed down.

"Yeah, OK, just be a robot," Evans said. "Be a robot. There are a couple of people who are always going to say that. At the end of the day, Twitter is an avenue to express your own opinions, whether or not they align with your club's views or your city's views. They're still your own."

Perhaps inevitably, then, given his background and ability to speak his mind, Evans took over as the team's players' union representative when Taylor Graham retired in 2010.

"I wanted to make a difference," Evans said, and when the league's collective bargaining agreement expired following the 2014 season, he finally got his opportunity.

Ask any longtime league observer, especially former players from the first few years of the league's existence, and they've all got stories like Evans's parable of the pay stub.

Lagerwey, the 150th pick of the inaugural MLS draft, remembers how, when he was with the Dallas Burn, the changing room was a double-wide trailer parked in the parking lot of a local middle school: "We had to schedule practices around recess." At least that Dallas team had a regular field. When Lagerwey was in Kansas City that first year, in 1996, the unfortunately named Wiz would train in whichever public park had an open field on any given morning.

Carlos Bocanegra, the longtime U.S. international who later became Atlanta United's first sporting director, recalls playing in the cavernous Cotton Bowl in front of two thousand fans, if he's being generous, and in high school football stadiums that were at least appropriate for the crowd sizes but still had the end zones painted from the previous Friday night.

"We stayed in hotels that were more like motels, where the doors are on the outside with the parking lot in the middle," Bocanegra said, shaking his head at the memory.

They've all got them, vivid tales of paltry salaries and cheap, greasy team meals and fleabag motels. They were professional in name only, closer to semi-pro than they were to athletes in the other major North American leagues.

The officially sanctioned explanation from the league was that limiting expenses was the only way to survive its first decade. Major League Soccer learned much — perhaps too much — from the ghost story of the NASL, where legends like Pele and Franz Beckenbauer once plied their trade, which collapsed under the weight of its own overspending.

MLS formed as a single entity, in which instead of running as independently operated teams, they're all technically owned and controlled by the league's investors. This chosen format begged all sorts of questions — competitive nature most of all — and the league was actually taken to court by its players via an antitrust lawsuit that it ultimately won in 2000.

Legitimate criticism aside, the structure accomplished its primary goal of controlling operating costs and discouraging a cutthroat free-for-all among its members. MLS wobbled unsteadily through its first 10 years, folding the Miami and Tampa Bay franchises in 2002. Even as its lot steadily improved throughout that decade, and especially in the early part of the next, its leadership group was hesitant to turn against its original, conservative nature.

MLS commissioner Don Garber once articulated his goal of turning the league into one of the world's best by 2022. Probably overly ambitious in the first place, rhetoric wasn't always backed up by tangible actions behind the scenes. As much as MLS had grown since Evans's first season in 2007, players were still often reminded of the disconnect between the league's Major League name and their day-to-day realities.

Teams were limited to just a few charter flights each per season. That meant flying commercial, which meant cramped middle seats on cross-country flights, which meant tight muscles and games that were sometimes delayed because of weather complications holding up away teams. The Designated Player rule improved the lot for a select few, but as recently as 2014, even as guys like Brazilian superstar Kaka ($7.2 million in annual guaranteed compensation) and Dempsey ($6.7 million) raked in the big bucks, the league minimum still sat at $36,500 per year.

A snowstorm threatened Washington, D.C., as Major League Soccer's players' union representatives and the league's owners descended on the nation's capital in late February of 2015. With the start of the new season just a few weeks away and the specter of a work stoppage looming like those dark clouds on the horizon, time was of the essence.

A boardroom had been set aside for the players' reps, more than 40 of them from various rivals crowding around a long mahogany table. Union executive director Bob Foose and general counsel Jon Newman kicked things off with a general presentation hitting on the most pressing issues, interrupted here and there by opinions from around the room. The topics ranged from guaranteed salaries for rookies to Designated Player thresholds for the biggest stars, from the daily per diem for meals on the road to the quality of hotels for visiting teams. Most of them were pitifully low for a league of such grandiose public ambitions.

The rules of order were a bit of a mess. There were 30-minute breaks every so often for guys to check back in with their teammates and solicit general consensus. Evans, who was Seattle's only rep on hand, burned through all of his available cell phone minutes in less than four days.

"It wasn't as organized as it should have been," Evans said. "It was kind of organized chaos. But it was chaos."

That the deck was stacked against the players was obvious from the outset. The union was formed in 2003 in the aftermath of *Fraser v. Major League Soccer*, the antitrust lawsuit that had gone in the league's favor. Whereas similar unions in Major League Baseball, for example, have been around for more than 50 years and employ staffs of more than 100, the MLS union had six full-time employees heading into the 2015 talks.

"Nobody was experienced enough in sports labor negotiations to know how to get what we wanted," Evans said. "We've never won anything. Minimal things, yeah, but we hadn't really ever had a 'win,' per se, in a labor dispute."

They gradually landed on a list of demands, foremost among them a minimum salary of $100,000 and free agency — that the ability to negotiate with other teams at contract's end was up for debate showcased how far they still had to go. When Evans sat next to USMNT captain Michael Bradley and across the table from Commissioner Garber and a selection of owners to pitch their proposal, he felt a surge of both personal pride and optimism. It was short-lived.

Management essentially dismissed the offer out of hand, coming back with a rebuttal so one-sided that the players voted by an 18–1 margin (with one abstention) to go on strike. This was late Tuesday night, with the season set to kick off that Friday. For a moment, at least, the first work stoppage in MLS history seemed like a genuine possibility.

Then the players started to fracture. The league's salary structure was so stratified that those at the bottom could hardly afford a few weeks — let alone months — without pay, while some toward the top were interested more in eking out every last dollar than labor solidarity. There was also a divide between the rank-and-file lifers and the stars who had come to MLS only recently.

Jacob Peterson from Sporting Kansas City, who came into the league one year before Evans and on a similarly puny starting salary, advocated striking no matter what.

"He was another player like me who had been screwed over in the start of his career, so he was like, 'No. I'm willing to sit for six, seven, eight games, a year, to see what it takes to make these guys budge,'" Evans said.

Others considered taking even the first counterproposal just to get it over with and back on the field. The goal of a six-figure minimum was all well and good, but those that would've been affected — those still just trying to break in and typically without much seniority — were underrepresented.

"You get down to the deadline, and there are guys in the room that are making $600 [thousand] or $700 and want to make $800 or $900," Evans said. "They want that money for themselves. It gets really difficult, and guys start to butt heads a bit. We thought we could accomplish what we set out to accomplish, but we just had a very bad setup or plan coming into it, and MLS ate us alive."

The new CBA passed, but the verdict was far from unanimous — seven teams voted against the terms of the deal that was agreed on in principle less than 48 hours before the campaign kicked off — and the players' gains were rife with caveats.

Sure, they'd won a form of free agency, but only for players 28 or older who had been in the league for at least eight years, and with raises capped at 25 percent. The minimum salary was raised to $60,000, not chump change but also far from the original goal. Charter flights, too, remained capped, locking in long trips in coach for at least five years.

For a league on the upswing, whose expansion fees alone would balloon to more than $100 million over the next few years, it was fair to conclude that the union would need to wait until 2020 for that long-sought first legitimate labor "win." It was obvious, too, that by the terms of the agreement, MLS would have to wait another long five years before it really began to make serious strides toward becoming one of the world's top leagues.

Given how rattled he was, Evans did a double take to make sure the women doing yoga in the middle of the airport terminal in Minneapolis were real, not some sort of exhaustion-provoked mirage. Halfway home from D.C. and waiting for his connection, Evans still felt anxious, his heartbeat trilling away in his chest. Not sure what else to do, he joined in the full yoga session before boarding the flight to Seattle-Tacoma, conspicuous in his lack of tights and mat. That helped, temporarily at least.

"Mentally, emotionally, it was the most draining thing I'd ever done," Evans said of the CBA talks.

It wasn't just the perceived loss in negotiations. It was the weight of the responsibility that he'd willingly yoked onto his own shoulders. He'd wanted to help his fellow players to better lives, and on some level, he felt as though he failed. Whereas other teams had multiple representatives on hand to pore over the fine print and bounce ideas off each other, Evans stood alone. Whether real or imagined, he sensed that some Sounders teammates blamed him for the group letdown.

Once he returned to Seattle, Evans took a step back. He relinquished his role as player rep and said he would be keeping opinions to himself for the foreseeable future. This went beyond the immediate sting of disappointment. It also tapped into the Darwinian power structure of professional sports. Evans was getting older, and his position on the Sounders depth chart was less secure than it once was. He didn't possess the leverage he once did.

Moving forward, 2016 proved a trying year for Evans, even if it would end on a high note. He just couldn't seem to stay healthy. He would tweak a groin, then a calf. Through most of summer and autumn, he was tormented by what team doctors thought was a calf strain that would turn out to actually be a herniated disk in his back. For the first time in a long time, he was forced to consider the end of the road.

As such, his tongue loosened back up toward the beginning of the following year. He was a realist, but not a cynic. Breaking down the impact of the CBA a couple years on, he was less downbeat than he was originally.

"Really in the last couple of years, everything has bumped up a little," Evans said. "You're always going to have the guys making the minimum that feel like they're getting screwed, but that's just the reality of it. That'll change in the next 10 years or so."

The players' standing would only get stronger as the league continued its upward trajectory, as Evans saw it, for reasons not all that dissimilar to why the union had struggled in 2015: internal divisions.

It's simplistic but helpful to break the ownership group in half, between the old and new guard. While the New England Krafts and Dallas Hunts still fought tooth and nail to keep costs at a bare minimum, a new wave of ambitious upstarts was beginning to make its collective voice heard. That process began with Toronto and Seattle and has continued in Orlando and Atlanta. As MLS continued to expand — demanding expansion fees that attracted only potential owners who were willing to spend extravagantly — the balance was beginning to tilt in one particular direction.

"I think they're very divided," Evans said. "And I think the guys that aren't going to spend are going to get weeded out real quick. The guys that are willing to spend are going to overpower them quickly. Once the Hunts are out of it, I think you're going to see a big shift."

(The irony was that, once upon a time, the Hunt family actually saved MLS. In November of 2001, FC Dallas president and co-owner Dan Hunt later claimed, the league had essentially decided to cease operations until his father, Lamar, stepped in. With the Miami and Tampa Bay clubs both in the throes of death, documents were being prepared to seal the league's fate until Lamar rallied support to keep things going.)

Times, though, had changed. At some point, the league was going to need to decide whether to loosen the purse strings and have an actual go at becoming one of the world's best leagues or accept perpetual mediocrity. Those with grander visions of what the original owners thought was possible were beginning to win the day.

"I got a sense for that during negotiations," Evans said. "Being in meetings with owners that were in there, you could see some that were kind of looking away when the Hunts would talk, and when Mark Abbott would talk, shaking their heads a little bit. It's definitely there, they just need to have that group together enough to push back against the league.

"I think that we'll get there eventually."

SIX

In its native Dutch, the surname *Lagerwij* means "lower meadow."

Hailing mostly from Utrecht, in central Holland, and the area around it, the clan wasn't particularly prosperous, but it was proud. All it took was a couple of pen marks made by an indifferent immigration officer to wipe generations of history clean. Either purposefully or accidentally, the last name was forever Anglicized when the family arrived at Ellis Island outside New York in the 1910s — thereafter, they were the Lagerweys.

Garth Lagerwey's great-grandparents did not arrive on these shores with much material wealth. Then as now, immigrants to the New World rarely did. What the couple brought over was a keen sense of sacrifice, as well as an indomitable work ethic. During those lean first years, those virtues went a long way.

Walter, Garth's grandfather, recalled walking barefoot during frigid winters, first in New York and later in Grand Rapids, Michigan. Shoes were not a luxury the family could afford. Walter picked up a paper route to help out, pedaling his bike down deserted early-morning streets. For his labor, he was rewarded with a nickel per week — all of which went toward that month's rent payment, eternally the cause of much consternation within the household.

Walter was drafted into the United States Army during World War II, serving in England as an interpreter for the Dutch Resistance. Thanks to his service, he qualified for a college scholarship through the GI Bill, becoming the first member of the Lagerwey/Lagerwij clan to receive post-secondary education. He went on to become a professor of Dutch at Calvin College in Grand Rapids. He wrote one of the first Dutch-English textbooks to be published in the United States. If his chosen field was a bit obscure, perhaps, so was it safe and stable. In the wider arc of his family's story, this represented an indisputable step forward.

His eldest, Wallace, heard all the stories from the Old Country to the new, from the lean times to the more comfortable ones. He observed his father closely, as a son does, internalizing the lessons of his life story even if he didn't recognize it as such at the time. Wallace trod a parallel path to his father's, similar if not step for step. He also devoted himself to the study of a foreign language, but it was German, not Dutch.

Wallace became a professor at Elmhurst College on the outskirts of Chicago and went on to earn his Ph.D. from Northwestern. He married his dream girl and bought a house in a nice neighborhood. Wallace eventually came to head up all of Elmhurst's foreign language programs and persuaded the college to start an international studies program he himself took charge of. Through that last posting he became a globetrotter, scouring continents for potential student and professor exchange programs.

"He created, basically, his dream job, which allowed him to travel all over the world," said his eldest, Garth, in whose mind that idea slowly germinated.

The expectation was there in the background even if it was

never articulated. Those decades of sacrifices for gradual, marginal gains were to be carried forward and paid off.

And so Garth was not only to create his very own dream job but also to succeed wildly in it. Thus was progress made, and if this wasn't the Sounders general manager's only or even primary motivation, it was always there, somewhere toward the back of his brain.

"It's the progression of my family," Lagerwey said. "My dad kind of took that to another level for our family, and hopefully I'm moving things forward. It's kind of like a responsibility to what comes after you, I guess."

When Lagerwey was 17 years old, his father made him an offer that he wouldn't realize the full significance of until years later. With the fall of the Berlin Wall, an opportunity had opened up for Wallace to travel around the former East Germany for a year doing cultural studies. Would his son like to go along and see if he could make a go of it abroad as a professional soccer player?

This offer was not made lightly, nor was it the product of overbearing parents forcing their child against his will toward sporting glory. Lagerwey's mother, Marcia, was also an educator, an elementary school teacher in nearby Bensonville. Few things were as paramount in the Lagerwey household than the value of an education — something Wallace and Marcia backed up with action as well as with stern words.

"The good news was, they were willing to mortgage the house to pay for college, if necessary," Lagerwey said. "The bad news was that any possible path other than college was not going to be tolerated. Of course, I rebelled against that."

It was only after he sufficiently proved his devotion to the game, and flashed a talent that could actually take him places, that his parents started to yield.

"If you really want to do the soccer thing before you go to college," Wallace asked Garth, and note the qualifier at the end of that phrase, "why don't you come to Germany with me and we'll try to find you a team?"

By picking up from his job to support his son's dreams, Wallace was betting on him another way, a type of parental devotion he hoped to eventually pay forward to his own sons. Garth caught on with a fourth-division team — "glamorous stuff, I assure you," he said — and stayed with a host family while his father traveled around the eastern part of the country.

Midway through his stay there, Lagerwey tore his Achilles, sidelining him for the duration of the trip. It was a setback, to be sure, but he still embraced the cultural immersion. The injury gave him a wider perspective he carried with him to Duke University and later Major League Soccer. For the first time, he began to consider a life without soccer at its core.

"Some of my teammates who played with me in the pros probably think I should've reached that conclusion long before that," he liked to joke.

After four years with the Blue Devils and a spell with the delightfully named and minor-league New Orleans Riverboat Gamblers, Lagerwey was drafted in the 15th round, 150th overall, in the inaugural MLS Draft.

"I was the soccer version of Mr. Irrelevant," Lagerwey said, but he stayed at it, bouncing from Kansas City to Dallas to Miami before being cut by the Fusion in 2000. "For all five years that I played, I was the lowest surviving draft pick in the league. I did, in that sense, take some pride that I was at least playing to my talent ability, which probably wasn't very high."

If some players are cast adrift at the end of their playing careers, Lagerwey was always multifaceted enough to reinvent himself — it just took him a little while to figure out where to best deploy his talents. He became a guest columnist for *Sports Illustrated* and tried his hand at broadcast media. Eventually, perhaps inevitably, he reached back to the lessons ingrained in him from an early age. Higher learning beckoned him once more.

"My parents say that from the time I was old enough to speak, I was arguing with them and felt I should be treated on equal footing with the adults around me," Lagerwey said. "They always felt I was destined for law school."

In the fall of 2001, he enrolled in Georgetown Law.

It was during his seven years in the nation's capital that Lagerwey found himself, finally landing on a dream job that combined all his best attributes and aspirations. He would become a GM, combining his passion for pro sports with the legal and managerial expertise he'd picked up at Georgetown and Latham & Watkins.

"I got that idea from my dad — find a way to make the job you want — and it was inspiring that he figured out a way to do it," Lagerwey said. "You have to work hard to see the sunlight sometimes."

The perseverance required was an especially valuable lesson. Because while Lagerwey set up a series of sit-downs with sports executives once he landed on what he ultimately wanted to do, their mostly uniform advice was disheartening.

"There is no path," Lagerwey said. "There is no linear progression. 'I want to be a general manager.' Oh, great, so do five million other people."

The only way in was to get a fortuitous break, being in exactly the right place at precisely the right time. This was something that could not be forced.

While he waited, Lagerwey made the best of it. He met his wife, Hilary, thanks to a blind date set up by his future mother-in-law, a coworker at the law firm. They were mostly just humoring her, bringing groups of friends as backup and meeting at a seedy dive bar that served only light beer and green Jell-O shots, "to set the level of expectation," Lagerwey said. Hilary's support group arrived drunk from an earlier birthday party, and the bulk of them were thrown out for starting a fight, giving him his opening.

"She says that's the only reason we got married, because she was forced to talk to me," Lagerwey said.

Professionally, too, he progressed in leaps and bounds. If some might have looked at him cockeyed for speaking so fondly of his corporate law firm, he really did cherish the opportunity it afforded and the methods he learned.

The firm encouraged his ancillary projects as well. When he landed the Real Salt Lake gig after that fortuitous assignment over Christmas 2006, the higher-ups offered to help negotiate his contract. Earlier, they allowed him to take a leave of absence to work on a political campaign back in his native Illinois against popular incumbent governor Rob Blagojevich — this was before Blagojevich's first corruption charge hit, mind you — and Lagerwey's team "just got slaughtered," he recalled.

In sum, he drew inspiration from a wealth of experiences when RSL finally came calling in 2007. Through his time as a professional himself, he understood locker room dynamics. He knew how to work with the media thanks to his spell with *SI* and on TV, and he learned the value of organizational culture and management methods through his time at Latham.

Progression wasn't always linear, for individuals or families as a whole. Even if one is convinced they're ready for their big chance earlier on, often that chance comes just at the right time.

"You don't know along the way what's going to benefit you, and what's going to help you," Lagerwey said. "This job is kind of perfect for me."

If the gig was a snug fit, so was Salt Lake City the ideal staging ground for Lagerwey's new career. Sheltered from expectations by the club's lack of previous accomplishments and from peering outside eyes by Utah's isolation, he and Kreis were given a rare gift in professional sports: the freedom to experiment and to fail — at least at first, until they found their footing. Launched in 2005, RSL had never even sniffed the postseason until the duo's first full season in charge, in 2008.

"Honestly, we tried stuff," Lagerwey said — styles, formations, all kinds of different player combinations. "There was nothing there to break. All the china was shattered on the floor. We were just trying to put teacups together."

He and Kreis had known each other for nearly 20 years at that point, having first met at a soccer camp in Austin, Texas, as boys. They played together at Duke, growing so close that Lagerwey actually slept on Kreis's parents' couch when the two were slumming it in the minor leagues with the Riverboat Gamblers. Their partnership ensured mutual trust. It was illustrative that as much as Lagerwey may have preferred a hands-off approach, it wasn't always easy to separate the personal from the business side when tough decisions needed to be made.

"There were lots of times where I literally could not be in the same room with him during the years we were at Real Salt Lake," Kreis said. "The stresses and strains of doing that type of job with somebody is such that there are going to be moments where you don't like each other very much. I would say it's almost like being married. There are moments where you don't like your wife very much, and there are going to be some really nasty fights. At the end of the day, you still love each other. I would say the same thing about Garth."

Gradually, eventually, those moments of nastiness gave way to unparalleled success for a club of RSL's size within MLS. Having turned over nearly three-fourths of the roster during Lagerwey's first three transfer windows, Salt Lake reached the Western Conference final in 2008 and won the league championship a year later.

Far from satiated, Lagerwey and Kreis never stopped tinkering. In some ways, they were the beneficiaries of MLS's mediocrity-rewarding playoff system — their career record was still actually below .500 when they first won the MLS Cup, and the 2009 team finished the regular season 11-12-7 before sneaking into the postseason and getting hot. That, and neither man was exactly the type to rest on his laurels anyway.

"We didn't take the wrong message from that [2009 championship]," Lagerwey said. "It comes back to humility. A lot of guys take the wrong message after one good year."

The 2011 team was probably RSL's best squad ever — and deserves to be held up there alongside the league's finest. With a core of players all hitting their respective peaks around the same time, and an oft-stated but rarely duplicated mantra that prized the collective over the individual, Salt Lake fell one away goal shy of becoming the first MLS club to win the CONCACAF Champions League.

Two years later, RSL reached another MLS Cup final, this time falling to Sporting Kansas City on penalty kicks. By that point, the sirens of brighter lights and larger markets were beginning to call. Less than a week after the loss to SKC, Kreis announced his intention to leave for an ill-fated stint with expansion New York City FC, a big-money collaboration of the Yankees and Manchester City of the English Premier League. A year later, Lagerwey left his post to take over as Seattle's GM and president of soccer. Some of what precipitated Salt Lake's breakup was inevitable. On some level, both Lagerwey and Kreis wanted to prove he could win without the other.

"Hugely, massively, overwhelmingly, powerfully," Lagerwey said when asked how much he was driven to succeed on his own. "It wasn't about being apart from J. We both had the same idea: if you can do this on the smaller scale, can you then replicate it on a bigger stage?"

Lagerwey was never shy about the size of his grand ambitions. *It's kind of like a responsibility to what comes after you.*

"Soccer is a cause, still," Lagerwey said. "It's still something we hope will grow and become this great thing that is the European Champions League and the World Cup. Even among general managers, we're all competitive, but we all want the entity to succeed and grow."

He wanted not only to win MLS Cups, and CONCACAF Champions Leagues, but also to make his own mark on the way the game is grown and cultivated within this country.

"The bigger stage piece was that you're not going to transform how you develop players in the United States while working for Salt Lake," Lagerwey said. "But if you can do the same thing working for Seattle, maybe that's now a scalable model. You know at Salt Lake that you're not going to change the world. But if you go to the Seattle Sounders, with 40,000 people in the building, maybe now you do have some influence. Maybe you can change the course of something or make the whole thing better."

Even during the best of times, the Sounders' annual Alliance Council business meetings could be tense affairs. Fans lined up to vent their frustrations with management, ranging from the frivolous (why aren't there more local craft beer options at CenturyLink) to the point-blank (is our coach going to keep his job).

The 2015 edition was to be especially strained — and would have lasting consequences on the club both in a short- and long-term sense. The meeting, hosted at the Paramount Theatre in downtown Seattle, took place just days after the Sounders had been run out of the playoffs by ascendant FC Dallas, and emotions were raw.

Owner Joe Roth got the evening off to a rousing start by confusing winger Marco Pappa's homeland of Guatemala with Nicaragua and then, when corrected by multiple shouts from the darkened audience, dismissing the gaffe by adding that both Central American countries were "cocaine distributors" anyway.

That would have likely stolen all the headlines in liberal Seattle if not for the breaking news to emerge later in the night, when Lagerwey clumsily revealed that Schmid would be returning as head coach for 2016. Lagerwey botched the big reveal of Schmid's return for the upcoming season when he called out into the darkened audience — further burying a subtle tweak of the club's bylaws that greatly benefitted the GM.

As part of the Sounders' unique structure of fan evaluation and control of front-office operations, every four years supporters voted to retain, or not retain, the team's general manager. It went back to one of the biggest drivers behind the success of the launch: empowering fans, giving them a voice and a tangible sense of ownership almost unique in North American sports.

The timing of Lagerwey's hire, after year six and midway through that quadrennial cycle, complicated this process. Should the fans vote to repeal him after his second season, in the fall of 2016, or give him a full cycle?

Amid the heated emotions of that particular evening, this was not an inconsequential question. Remember, at this point, the general manager wasn't all that popular with the fan base. Following up on two-trophy 2014, the most recent campaign had ended without silverware — worse, without even much of a push for any. The rift between Lagerwey and Schmid was mostly hidden from public view at that point, but still, asked to choose sides, support for the longtime coach would've been almost unanimous.

Plus, in the age of fantasy sports, few gigs invited constant scrutiny more than that of a GM's.

"I have the job that very few people have had and that everyone assumes they can do better than me," Lagerwey said. "It's not personal to me. That's just being the general manager."

The vote on the rule change nominally went in his favor, deciding that each four-year cycle would begin anew every time a new GM took over. There was one hell of a caveat built into the fine print, however: season-ticket holders still held the option to trigger a one-time recall vote just two years in.

All this parliamentary mumbo jumbo is to put into full context the organizational tug-of-war throughout 2016. Schmid felt the pressure more acutely as the losses started to mount, but if Lagerwey was on a slightly more protracted deadline, he, too, felt an internal hourglass slowly emptying of sand.

Fear of failure was another powerful motivator. He couldn't bring to fruition his audacious plans for advancing his beloved sport in his home country — let alone pay tribute to his ancestors and advance his extended family's cause — if he was unceremoniously thrown out onto his ass after just a few seasons at one of MLS's leading clubs.

"That's always there," Lagerwey said. "Maybe I'm twisted, but I actually think it's healthy, on some level. I was a guy in college who would procrastinate papers, but at the end of the day, if you didn't write them, you didn't graduate. You'd stay up all night to write the paper. It was only the fear of failure that actually put your fingers on the keyboard."

So Lagerwey dug his heels in as forces aligned against him in greater numbers over the first half of 2016. It wasn't just the coaching staff that pressed for reinforcements — even casual observers could identify what ailed the Sounders. They struggled to score, but they weren't playing *badly*, per se. They would dominate possession for long stretches of matches yet look flummoxed every time they neared an opposing box.

"I think maybe a few players were getting frustrated," defender Tyrone Mears said.

"It wasn't anything to do with the training, the tactics. We were just crying out for a playmaker. We were all saying it, that that's what we desperately needed."

Seattle had the means to line up a signing as soon as the summer transfer window opened on July 10, the day after the disheartening 1–0 loss to Los Angeles at home but before the consecutive disasters in Portland and Kansas City later that month.

Lagerwey, though, was fixated on one particular potential acquisition. If Schmid had helped establish the initial connection with Nicolas Lodeiro — as evidenced by how warmly the player commiserated with the coach on the way out — it was the general manager who held steadfast on the Uruguayan as the club's number one target. Lodeiro personified Lagerwey's vision for the future of the Sounders: young, dynamic and out of South America, where the GM had mined so much talent while at RSL.

Seattle's pursuit was complicated by Boca Juniors' deep, pesky run in the Copa Libertadores. The Argentine powerhouse was loath to sell their playmaker in the midst of a push for the continental championship. In a butterfly-flaps-its-wings kind of way, there's an alternative universe in which Boca falls to Nacional on penalty kicks in the quarterfinals in mid-May, rather than the other way around, and Lodeiro lands in Seattle at the beginning of July. Instead, the Sounders were made to wait.

With the players and even parts of the coaching staff pushing for expedited alternatives, Lagerwey held fast. If he was going to fail, he was going to do so on his own terms.

Lodeiro arrived too late to save Schmid's job but just in time to rescue the season. Lagerwey would finally have the opportunity to build the team he saw fit, the opportunity he'd been striving for in various ways for as long as he could remember.

SEVEN

IN EARLY OCTOBER OF 2016, Adrian Hanauer sat on a lime-green couch in his corner office at the club's Pioneer Square headquarters and laid out his vision for its near- and long-term future.

The building itself spoke much about the Sounders' — and Hanauer's — aspirations. Splitting business operations from the Seahawks in early 2014 was a leap into the unknown. That partnership had been fruitful, and why mess with a good thing? Hanauer and the rest of the franchise brass, however, were convinced they would never reach their full potential until they struck out on their own.

There had been hiccups early on, acrimonious breaks with longtime employees and questions about whether they could invest in the same way without the backing of an NFL team. And yet this space was undoubtedly their own. With exposed walls of Pioneer Square's distinctive red brick, open floor plans and millennials scrolling through smartphones, Sounders HQ felt like a tech start-up when compared with the Seahawks' more staid offices in the suburbs.

Hanauer was justifiably proud of this tableau and at home here, reclining slightly with his elbows resting atop the couch's lip. But the majority owner was far from content with what had already been achieved, instead consumed by big-picture questions of where it all went from there.

That October afternoon was also the first time Hanauer had spoken publicly about his decision to fire Schmid a few months prior. And as much as he insisted otherwise, the organizational blueprint he described and the jettisoning of the team's longtime coach were not entirely unrelated. Because while Seattle had been nose-diving on the field, in the background, Hanauer and the business team had been busy crafting an aspirational 10-year plan pinned around what they hoped would be a 2026 World Cup hosted jointly by the United States, Mexico and Canada.

The process had been in the works for a while up to that point. The split from the Seahawks was an opportune time for internal soul-searching. In sketching out possible initiatives, the Sounders cast a wide net, interviewing its own players, coaches and fans, as well as front-office types from around the league, seeking as diverse a range of opinions as possible.

"The formal process started in 2015, but even before that, we were talking about who we wanted to be as an organization," Hanauer said. "What are our big, audacious goals?"

By the summer of 2016, a rough draft shortlist of strategic objectives had come into shape. Some were mind-numbingly bureaucratic sounding: continue to evolve and focus on democracy in sport; engage, lead and serve in the community; run a "responsible and sustainable" business. Others were easier to define and thus more compelling: win (multiple) MLS Cups, and sell out the entirety of CenturyLink Field's 67,000 capacity for every game within the next decade.

The timing was important. The split necessitated some level of introspection, to be sure, but there was more to it than that. After improving in leaps and bounds during the first few seasons from the low 30,000s to the mid 40,000s, attendance had mostly flatlined in recent years. Those numbers were none too shabby, ranking favorably even in some of the top leagues in the world, but any kind of stagnation was a red flag, especially when large chunks of the upper deck remained empty for most home games.

Of greater immediate concern, the team was on track for its lowest average attendance figure since the beginning of the decade — indeed, even after things stabilized following the coaching change, Seattle would post its lowest figure since 2011. This was not the only measure of the club's overall health, but in a league still struggling for television ratings, butts in seats was still the preeminent metric.

Hanauer planned on rolling out the 10-year plan at the annual Alliance Council business meeting. What had originally been planned as a triumphal moment in the club's history would take on an altogether different vibe if it came at the tail end of the worst campaign in the team's modern era.

Hanauer usually spoke carefully. His cadence was slow, and he sometimes stopped to edit himself midsentence in order to make sure he was expressing himself just right. That autumn at team HQ, the sun slowly setting outside the windows, Hanauer was more forthright. He spoke plainly and emotionally, the typically controlled and bespectacled owner giving a glimpse at how the year had personally affected him.

On Schmid's firing, he didn't hold back: "I think the team was done hearing him," Hanauer said. "We have different perspectives on it. He could be right, I could be wrong. But it was my conclusion that the team had — I don't want to say that the team had given up on him, because the team has pride — but that the messaging was not getting through."

Was he afraid the Sounders were plateauing? "It's woken me up in the middle of every night for the last eight and a half years," Hanauer said. "I'm paranoid about the ability for us to continue to grow the business and grow the sport. We can't let that [plateau] happen."

That paranoia shaped the events of the 2016 season perhaps more so than any other impulse, as the Sounders strove desperately to hold onto their slipping status as MLS's sexiest brand. New challengers to that title had been cropping up with regularity in recent years, and Seattle needed a change. Reinvention was necessary and had in fact been ongoing behind the scenes for years. Schmid's departure was only one part of the puzzle.

Joe Roth was looking for new worlds to conquer. Born in New York City, Roth made his name in Hollywood. The former chairman of both 20th Century Fox and Walt Disney Studios, he'd overseen a string of hit movies that included *Major League, Home Alone, Die Hard 2, My Cousin Vinny* and *White Men Can't Jump*.

By 2007, when a deal of his with Sony expired and allowed him to take a step back from a business he'd given several decades of his life to, Roth had made enough money to retire comfortably several times over. Instead, according to *Authentic Masterpiece*, a chronicle of the Sounders' launch, Roth woke up one morning and told his wife, Irene: "You know what? I think I'm going to start a soccer team."

Roth was an impulsive, creative type — that would become important later on down the line — but this particular bit of inspiration didn't come completely out of the blue. He played as a kid, and something about the game never left him. He was frustrated that soccer hadn't made the gains in the United States he thought it should have, and he figured there was an underexploited market there to be tapped. Through mutual friends, he was connected with Commissioner Garber. Roth explored all three Cascadian cities but was especially taken with Seattle.

At first glance, Roth and Hanauer were a mismatched coupling.

They first met at the 2007 MLS All-Star Game in Denver at the suggestion of Garber. Nobody had a better read on the Seattle soccer market at that time than Hanauer, and it was crucial to maintain some kind of local connection. Roth, though, forever the brash New Yorker, told Hanauer straight up that he was only interested if he could become the majority owner. (They would reverse roles later on down the line.) Hanauer could have bristled, given the years and funds sunk into the minor-league team that laid so much groundwork, but to his credit, he didn't.

On some level, they meshed. Roth was the big-money guy, the ideas guy, Mr. Hollywood. Hanauer was happy to cede some level of control in order to bring MLS to his hometown, and he played the role of the pragmatist, keeping Roth's more grandiose schemes in check.

The rest of the ownership group checked various additional boxes. Paul Allen, the Microsoft cofounder and owner of both the Seahawks and the NBA's Portland Trail Blazers, would take on 25 percent of the club in exchange for the Seahawks' business ops. Drew Carey, the charismatic host of daytime TV's *The Price is Right*, was brought on as the perpetually smiley face of the new franchise.

The rest, as the old chestnut goes, was history. With Gary Wright and Seahawks CEO Tod Leiweke pulling various levers in the background, the launch went off without a hitch. More than 30,000 fans poured into CenturyLink for opening night against the Red Bulls, and they never stopped coming.

The Sounders won the U.S. Open Cup in each of the first three years of their existence, finishing in the top four in the Western Conference and qualifying for the MLS playoffs in each of those seasons. They reached the conference finals and the semifinals of the CONCACAF Champions League in 2012.

There was nowhere to go, it seemed at the time, but up.

If it is instructive to break the history of MLS into parts 1.0, 2.0 and 3.0, so it is helpful to envision the modern era of the Sounders as pre- and post-Seahawks. The years prior to 2014 were something of a prolonged honeymoon. Backed by the brand awareness and infrastructure of an NFL team, having struck all the right notes on the soccer side, too, the Sounders could seemingly do no wrong.

So why mix it up? For starters, the joint business operations were never meant to last forever. When the Sounders launched, the Seahawks didn't double their staff — they just piled double the work onto the backs of their existing employees. It was a testament to the leadership abilities of Leiweke, Wright and others to inspire excitement about the new venture that the setup lasted as long as it did.

By the five-year mark, the strain was beginning to show. Back-to-back Seahawks Super Bowl runs in 2013 and '14 pushed into mid-February, weeks before the MLS season started, cutting vacation time down to nearly nonexistent.

So the Sounders struck out on their own. The decision, announced on March 20, 2014, was abrupt enough that some of the Sounders' traveling employees, en route to a match in Montreal, didn't find out about it until their phones were collectively bombarded upon landing. Overnight, and perhaps to a greater extent than the decision-makers realized, economic realities shifted drastically.

"The Sounders kind of reminded me of a 21-year-old kid with a car and a girlfriend and a job," said Mike Gastineau, author of *Authentic Masterpiece*. "Mom and Dad eventually say, 'Guess what? It's time to start living on your own.' It feels like maybe they took a step back, business-wise. Like a 21-year-old moving out, they didn't quite realize everything that was going to be on their dime. 'Wait a minute, I get an electric bill every month? What?' It wasn't quite that naive, but there were things that came along that they could not have expected because they were sheltered for so long."

Thus a franchise that liked to talk a big game about the scale of their ambitions was forced to take a long look at what was possible independently. Publicly, Hanauer insisted that nothing at all had changed. Internally, the club was forced to cut some corners. Multiple employees who experienced the transition referred to the shift as going from NFL-lite to MLS-plus. Expenses were trimmed, and staff turned over at a high rate.

"Joe and I have basically said from day one that we have no interest in pulling cash out of the operations of the business, but we don't want to write checks either," Hanauer said. "There's a reality of striking a balance. That's why we didn't commit $40 million to a player. There are decisions and trade-offs to be made.

"Sometimes you have to make decisions between new carpeting for the office or a technology solution for scouting players. We're going to err on the side of doing whatever we can to support the team and the team's success. That will be the biggest driver of revenue and success that will ultimately circle back and provide the resources to change the carpet."

An identity crisis, on some level at least, was inevitable.

Even postsplit, Don Garber was nothing short of effusive in his praise for the Sounders as his league's model franchise.

"We realized very, very quickly that this team would break the mold," the MLS commissioner said. "It really made a very strong statement that MLS is a league on the rise. The potential is limitless. The Sounders are the showcase for our league when we're looking at new investors. The first place they visit is Seattle. The second place they visit is Portland.

"They are the showcase brand."

Those weren't empty words: look no further than the waves of expansion that followed for evidence of Seattle's impact on Major League Soccer as a whole. Despite having for so long dragged its feet in making its way Northwest, the league granted franchises to both Portland and Vancouver shortly after the Sounders' debut, with both teams entering prior to the 2011 season.

Whitecaps owner Bob Lenarduzzi said Seattle's spectacular early gains didn't directly come up during negotiations — because it was such an obvious influence that it was taken for granted.

"I don't even think it needed to be discussed," Lenarduzzi said. "The league didn't need reminding. Just look three hours down the road, and even if we don't get the same numbers in attendance that they did, there's still a huge base of support in Vancouver and likewise in Portland. It's great that Seattle had done as well as they had done, and it definitely helped Portland and us."

Both the 'Caps and Timbers followed a familiar model. Each moved into stadiums near their respective city centers, and each targeted demographics that the Sounders had so successfully homed in on. Just as important, both of the other Cascadian clubs built on the legacies of their NASL franchises and successive minor-league teams that kept the flame of the game alive before the arrival of MLS.

The blueprint was successfully mimicked even in markets with less in common. New York City FC and Orlando, which both entered the league in 2015, added their own fresh twists, but there were notable similarities.

Backed by a partnership between the Yankees and Manchester City of the EPL, NYCFC benefitted from its cash-heavy support system and tapped into a similar demographic in the Big Apple. Orlando stayed close to downtown, first at the Citrus Bowl and then at its own eye-catching new home, and sought to encourage a distinctive supporters' culture. The new stadium came complete with a standing terrace, the first in a North American stadium, to add to the atmosphere.

Atlanta most closely followed the Seattle model — and, not coincidentally, would quickly established itself as the leading threat to the Sounders' standing as what Garber referred to as the "showcase brand."

Atlanta United FC, which was to debut at the beginning of the 2017 season, was owned by Falcons owner Arthur Blank and would also share resources and a stadium with an NFL team. Atlanta was so committed to learning from Seattle's experience that it sent a delegation of 10 staffers to spend a half-day at the Seahawks offices and a half-day at Sounders HQ in Pioneer Square shortly after they were awarded an expansion team.

"I can remember still being an executive in the Premier League," said Atlanta club president Darren Eales, formerly of Tottenham Hotspur and West Bromwich Albion, "and being surprised when the numbers came in from Seattle. It helped the league, from a national and international perspective, to get recognition. Seattle set the benchmark and helped the league get that notoriety abroad. I think what they did was they showed the direction. Almost accidentally, this model came together quickly. I think Toronto started that flame. I think Seattle brought it to a new level."

So who better to learn from? That one day Atlanta's brass spent bouncing between headquarters was far from the last bit of shared resources.

"Lord knows they lived in our offices for months," Hanauer said with a dry chuckle, putting a positive spin on the all-for-one ethos of MLS's collective ownership setup.

In 2017, Atlanta would become the first team since the Sounders entered MLS to overtake them in average attendance, topping out at more than 48,000 per game. Los Angeles FC was set to follow a year later as an expansion team with a deep-pocketed ownership group that included basketball icon Magic Johnson, Cardiff City owner Vincent Tan and movie star Will Ferrell.

In the fall of 2016, those future threats were still undefined, but it was possible to sense the rumblings. Those oncoming footsteps help to further explain the urgency within the Sounders front office. To keep up, they would need to at the very least check off the box that still eluded them on their overall resume.

"It's still a team in the MLS world that everyone looks at, at least part in admiration and even with a little bit of jealousy," ESPN analyst Taylor Twellman said of Seattle's standing during the latter part of 2016. "If Seattle ever can go on a championship type of run the way the L.A. Galaxy did, I think they're in the discussion for the best organization in Major League Soccer, top to bottom.

"They've set the bar so high with everything else, but they've yet to get to the MLS Cup. That's the missing piece."

Hanauer had a recurring nightmare in which he showed up to a Sounders game, took his seat up in his luxury box right before kickoff and looked out at an empty stadium. Even almost a decade into this project, when attendance that dipped into the 30,000s was considered a bad night, he was still never entirely sure whether they were going to recreate the magic on any given night.

"When it's 15 minutes before a game and the stands are still empty, I still worry if fans are going to show up," Hanauer said. "It's probably an unhealthy amount of paranoia and skepticism, but it's probably helpful, too, in not taking anything for granted."

That was the driving force between the shift in emphasis pre- and post-Seahawks.

The immediate success was oh so vital, as 2009 laid the groundwork for everything else that followed. A quick glance around MLS was enough to underline the importance of a strong first impression.

Yet the Sounders were not content with what they had already gained. Hanauer was desirous of more. That's why he initiated the split in business operations. That's why he ceded the GM role to Lagerwey, a divisive figure who the owner nevertheless believed was as intelligent an executive as any in the league. And that, yes, was the reason Hanauer fired Schmid despite a bond that had long since transcended the typical relationship between a coach and his boss.

"Just because something was done this way in the past doesn't mean this is how it's supposed to be done in the future, whether it's on the soccer side or on the business side," Hanauer said from his lime-green couch. "But we've been leaders from day one. There's a reason new franchises come and visit us still. It's not because of what we did eight years ago. It's because of what we're going to continue to do."

What, then, did the Sounders want to be, in the year 2016 and looking further ahead? Get your fingernails beneath the corporate-speak of those goals listed up in that first section — what did they actually mean?

Spend enough time at the Pioneer Square HQ and you'll hear the phrase *global brand* bandied about often. The club clearly had aspirations that pushed beyond the borders of Cascadia. That third bullet point — run a "responsible and sustainable" business — was also important to note and potentially contradictory to the aims of global dominion. Without the Seahawks' backing, the meaning of that line had changed.

"First of all, we are a global brand," Hanauer said. "When you're traveling around the world, if you see MLS gear, it's likely to be Sounders. When you hear people talk about what's going on in Major League Soccer, it's likely to be the Sounders. We absolutely want to be a global brand, but we have a lot of work to do: locally, regionally, nationally."

Locally. In order to conquer the world, the Sounders had to first establish a more secure foothold within their hometown. Their standing as one of the top teams in MLS was without question, even with Atlantas and LAFCs popping up to challenge them. Neither Garber nor Twellman was exaggerating: Seattle was a transformative influence within Major League Soccer and would remain so for the foreseeable future, even if it did scale back slightly behind the scenes.

Yet the Sounders were not the most popular sports team in Seattle itself. That designation unquestionably belonged to the Seahawks, whose presence was so all encompassing in the wake of their Super Bowl runs as to almost blot out the sun. Behind the Seahawks was the University of Washington football team, a historic West Coast power that had recently pulled out of a prolonged fallow period. Next still probably ranked the Mariners — the Sounders regularly outdrew the Ms in attendance, but TV ratings and regional relevance were another story.

To acknowledge those realities was not to suggest they would never change. Breaking into the mainstream takes time. Nostalgia is a powerful tool, and there's something to be said for the teams we followed in our youth, to the ones we pass down to our kids. Lingering memories of the NASL aside, the Seahawks, Mariners and Huskies each had decades-long head starts on the Sounders.

As much as his vision had widened over the years, Hanauer was still a local boy at heart. Seattle was where his family made its fortune as a high-end bedding manufacturer. It was where he grew up, where he went to school — first at Mercer Island High over on the Eastside and later at UW. It was where he caught his first soccer match inside the Kingdome, where he played the game for the first time, where he still played in adult men's leagues whenever he found a free night.

Hanauer was more aware than just about anybody exactly what notes his club needed to hit in order to burrow its way further into the local fabric. Name recognition and casual buzz were important, but so, too, was staying connected to grassroots.

That's part of why he was privately more bullish than most on Brian Schmetzer's chances of winning the head coaching gig on a full-time basis. It would ultimately be Lagerwey's call — Hanauer had been adamant about that from the get-go — but he and the interim coach had been close from their time spent together in the United Soccer League. Schmetzer could be underwhelming upon first impression, but the owner knew there was more to him than what met the eye.

"We're not going to pander to a demographic or make a decision for any other reason than helping us win," Hanauer said. "If we believe that Brian is the guy to help us win, then fantastic. And, by the way, there's a lot of familiarity with him. We know what a great cultural fit he is. We know what a great fit he is in the community. So for me, I would probably prefer — all things being equal on the overall coaching — I would lean toward community, culture and character than someone who is globally known.

"That goes the same for our players. Seattle, we're turning into a bigger city, but we're a little bit up here in the Northwest, counterculture, smaller-city attitude, and having big stars isn't that important to us. Having quality people is important."

Global brand versus local roots, making a splash versus trusting what you have — the clashing ideals of what the club saw in itself would be reflected in its search for Schmid's long term replacement. Whether or not Schmetzer could win the job for good would speak volumes of what the Sounders ultimately wanted to be, in 2016 and beyond.

EIGHT

ALAN HINTON RECLINED IN his leather office chair and ran a hand through his thick, curly blond hair. It was the summer of 1980, and the head coach of the Seattle Sounders had just received a distressing phone call. Pensively, he pondered his options.

Rookie midfielder Brian Schmetzer had signed his first professional contract just weeks earlier, and already he was in trouble. Schmetzer, barely 18 years old and fresh out of Nathan Hale High School on the north side of the city, had been on the way to a party with friends when he spotted a police cruiser out of the corner of his eye. He took a quick turn down a side street, but his reflexes were slowed by alcohol — they weren't quick enough.

Schmetzer wasn't arrested. He wasn't even charged. His punishment was even worse: the cops turned him over to his father, Walter, a stern disciplinarian who had coached Brian with a heavy hand ever since he was a boy.

Hinton wasn't quite as concerned. A former English international whose great Derby County teams bonded over many pints in the late '60s and early '70s, Hinton understood that teenagers do stupid things. He did, however, recognize the opportunity to put the fear of God into his new charge.

Standing in his office above FX McRory's in Pioneer Square with his back to the door, looking out at Puget Sound to his right and the Kingdome to his left, Hinton heard a knock. Walter came in first, practically dragging his son by the ear. Hinton theatrically pulled Schmetzer's freshly signed contract out of a file cabinet and dangled it in front of the teenager's face.

"What you've done is wrong," Hinton said in his gruff British accent. "You're not going to jail, or even getting fined. But that could have gotten into the newspaper, and linked you with the Sounders. That would have been embarrassing for the club, you understand?"

Schmetzer could only nod.

"So here's the deal," Hinton said. "If you get into this type of trouble again, you see that contract? I'm going to rip it up and you'll be out of here. I won't want you."

Hinton's message hit home. Years later, Schmetzer would refer to the meeting as a life-changing moment, the exact instant he realized what it would take to succeed as a pro. He had to grow up. If he wanted to make it, the time for messing around and making dumb mistakes with his high school buddies had come to an end.

It established an early beachhead in his mind about what it meant to be a Sounder. And it convinced Schmetzer — named the second head coach of the MLS Sounders in Schmid's wake — of the power of the face-to-face meeting, the hard-won détente. It informed perhaps the central principle of his own coaching philosophy.

Playing style was often fungible on Schmetzer's teams. Like Schmid, under whom he served as top assistant after leading the Sounders during the years prior to their ascension into MLS, Schmetzer molded his system to the players, rather than the other way around.

Schmetzer was not an immediately striking public speaker. His wife, Kristine, remembers being surprised the first time she watched him being interviewed at the charm that came through on camera. The Brian she knew was shy, the wallflower in most social settings. What Schmetzer did exceptionally well — what most close to him credited for his previous coaching successes, including two minor-league titles in three years — was connect with players one on one.

"Soccer players are funny," Schmetzer said. "Maybe funny isn't the right word, but I think they're pretty easy to manage within these guidelines: if you're honest with them, and tell them the truth even if it's not what they want to hear, you will be so far ahead of the game."

That was easier said than done, as Schmetzer found out in the days after he took over from Schmid, with the interim tag attached to his title.

Thirty-six years after his fateful meeting with Hinton, Schmetzer found himself sitting across from the player he referred to as "the greatest field player this country has ever produced," Clint Dempsey.

If the power structure was ostensibly reversed, Schmetzer in the coach's chair and Dempsey on the other side of the desk, it didn't exactly feel that way in the moment. Schmetzer's new reality hadn't sunk in yet, not really. The office he moved into was still scattered with Schmid's knickknacks and coaching tapes. A bobbleheaded Sigi peered accusingly around his computer monitor when he sat at his desk.

On the same July morning that Schmid gave his farewell address to the team, Schmetzer gave his first speech as interim head coach. Though the two men were as close as one could expect given their circumstance, with a shared German heritage and a similar sense of humor, and even though Schmetzer was temporarily gutted for the man who served as his mentor for seven-plus seasons, there wasn't much time to mourn.

That Tuesday, ahead of a nationally televised showdown with perennial powerhouse Los Angeles that coming weekend, Seattle was 10 points adrift of the playoff spots in the Western Conference. Though one might have expected some leeway, given the team's standing, Lagerwey made it clear that for a club that had never failed to qualify for the postseason, the playoffs were still the minimum expectation.

Schmetzer, in no uncertain terms, would be coaching for his job with little margin for error. The search for Schmid's full-time replacement, Lagerwey said, would begin immediately and would be wide ranging. For a club of Seattle's ambitions, that hinted heavily toward Europe.

Schmetzer got to work by leaning on his greatest strength, bringing in players one by one to set expectations. The sit-down with Dempsey, especially, was critical.

"It was significant in the sense that he was our best player," Schmetzer said.

One could make a case for the newly arrived Lodeiro, but Dempsey was still the locker room's alpha, "the big dog," as Schmetzer put it. He was the one the coach needed to win over if he were to have any shot of turning the season around.

"We're going to build the team around you," Schmetzer told him. "This is your team."

There were caveats, to be sure, about the need to fit into the team concept and sacrifice parts of himself for the greater whole, but the central message was clear: *We're going to build the team around you.*

Dempsey sat mostly impassively. The Texan could be hard to read. He mostly just stared, his face, as ever, set at a slight scowl. When Dempsey stood up to leave, Schmetzer wasn't totally sure whether he'd gotten through to his star. Dempsey, as has been his wont throughout his accomplished career, saved his answer for the pitch. After a 1–1 draw against the Galaxy, Seattle ripped off a three-match win streak, with Dempsey scoring five times in that trio of games.

The turnaround was off to a rip-roaring start, every win aiding the coach's task of winning the respect of his veterans. If Schmetzer thought he'd gotten the hardest part out of the way, though, he would soon be proven wrong.

On a typically dark and damp February night the following year, a group of Seattle soccer luminaries packed a wood-paneled British pub in the neighborhood of Ballard to near capacity.

The event, hosted by Washington State Legends of Soccer, was titled "Brian Schmetzer, This Is Your Life" and featured a panel of family members and former coaches, players and colleagues, each of whom took turns mixing sincere well wishes with gentle ribbing. The man of the hour was plainly mortified at being the center of such glowing attention — "awkward and embarrassing" were his first words to describe it. Though Schmetzer sat off to the side of the makeshift stage at the front of the room, perched uncomfortably atop a bar stool, he could feel the eyes of the entire room upon him.

He blushed red when the stories hit too close to home, like when grizzled Sounders defender Zach Scott recalled their minor-league days, when Schmetzer would throw him into games in the 89th minute to ensure he got the meager match-day bonus ($250) owed to him only if he saw the field. Schmetzer wiped away the occasional stray tear, too, such as ones shed when Jimmy Gabriel, one of his longtime mentors, described how proud he was of how far he'd come.

If the occasion was in honor of Schmetzer, it also underlined just how closely his own career path intertwined with the wider history of the sport in this city. Going all the way back to the days of his youth in the 1970s, Schmetzer played for or coached nearly every professional soccer team of significance in the greater Puget Sound.

Andy and Walt, Brian's brothers, waxed poetic about their exploits with the Lake City Hawks, the youth club their father coached that won multiple state championships. Schmetzer suited up for the NASL Sounders, of course, but played just as pivotal a role after that league went bust in 1983. He played for FC Seattle under the tutelage of Gabriel, a team semi-pro in nature but that had an outsized impact in keeping the flame of the game alive in the city.

The FC Seattle roster reads like a who's who of future coaches who would impact Washington State soccer for a generation. Everett native Chris Henderson would go on to a lengthy career with the U.S. national team before becoming the Sounders' sporting director. Pete Fewing went on to become the head coach at Seattle University, leading that program to multiple lower-division national titles and the Division I Sweet 16 in 2015. Chance Fry played a formative role with the youth club Eastside FC, which produced Morris, as did Bernie James at Crossfire, which played a huge role in the development of Yedlin.

Schmetzer was their guy, Seattle's guy. His fate, for good and for bad, was tied to the city's coaching fraternity, which knew exactly where he came from, and what he'd been through, to ascend to his current station.

After FC Seattle, Schmetzer played indoors for the San Diego Sockers and the Tacoma Stars and got his first taste of coaching as an assistant for the Seattle SeaDogs alongside Fernando Clavijo, later the sporting director of FC Dallas. Clavijo promised that the team would win a championship within three years — which it did, in 1997, a few weeks before their league folded. So it went for a soccer lifer in that particular time and place.

By the early 2000s, Schmetzer had settled into a rhythm. He worked full time in construction, coaching youth teams whenever he could find the time. He pitched in at the family sporting goods store. Thus, he didn't spare much of a thought when Hanauer, the new owner of the USL Sounders, left him a voice mail asking to meet up for coffee in early 2002. Schmetzer figured it was about the youth camps he'd been running, so he initially disregarded the message and then forgot to call Hanauer back. Luckily for him, his future boss was persistent. Hanauer tried again, asking to meet up for breakfast in Madison Park.

"Sure," Schmetzer texted back, "but only after I drop my kids off for school."

Hanauer was still relatively new to the management side of the Seattle soccer scene, so he picked the brains of every trusted contact he had within that tight-knit community, asking for advice about his coaching search. In conversation after conversation — many of them with folks who would later end up packed inside a wood-paneled bar one February night — one name in particular kept popping up.

Though they were originally supposed to meet only for a quick bite, the two men ended up talking for hours. Off the cuff, Schmetzer nailed the interview that would dramatically alter the trajectory of his career. A few days later, he was hired.

"I think I'm pretty good at judging character," Hanauer said, "and that was evident really early, that he had the right temperament, mentality, to rally the troops and be a good team leader."

Schmetzer's Sounders experienced mostly steady success. They won USL titles in 2005 and 2007, upsetting a couple of MLS clubs in U.S. Open Cup play along the way. Hanauer so believed in Schmetzer's coaching ability that he directly appealed to Schmid to bring him aboard as an assistant after the leap to MLS.

Still, it's not as though Schmetzer was anything more than a niche celebrity even in a region considered as soccer mad as Seattle.

A handful of years before the MLS jump and a decade or so before his biggest break, Schmetzer and Fewing were celebrating successful seasons with their families at a park up in Redmond. Fewing's Redhawks had just won the Division II national title, and Schmetzer's Sounders had also had a good year. They were feeling good about themselves, flush with pride but also fully aware of their place in the local sporting ecosystem — "glowing in our greatness," according to Fewing, "totally facetiously."

Schmetzer noticed a woman heading their way with camera in hand and sensed an opportunity to continue a running inside joke.

"Excuse me, ma'am," Schmetzer asked, wrapping his arm around his longtime colleague and buddy. "Do you want a photo?"

The stranger looked both of them up and down, making a snap judgment. She fired back with a response that underlined exactly where they stood at the time and which still brings a chuckle out of both men all these years later.

"Who in the hell," she sneered, "are *you*?"

Schmetzer was an easy man to underestimate. Based on appearances alone, with his wire-rimmed glasses and penchant for dad jeans, one would be far more likely to peg him as a high school algebra teacher than a top-level soccer coach.

He possessed a burning competitive drive — his ankle-biting exploits as a hard-nosed midfielder were evidence enough of that — but it often simmered deeply beneath the surface. His charisma didn't immediately light up rooms; he lacked the ego of many of his colleagues, like Schmid or Caleb Porter down in Portland. Whereas some coaches practically lived in their cramped little offices, Schmetzer prided himself on his work-life balance.

"When we go home, we have our life," Schmetzer said. "It's not ruled or dictated by soccer."

He and Kristine, who doesn't consider herself a soccer fan and couldn't recall the last time she watched a game not involving the

Sounders, religiously tuned in for *Jeopardy!* and played doubles tennis. They turned road matches into miniature vacations and looked for opportunities to unplug as often as possible — less often once he came to occupy the big chair.

All of that made for an exceptionally well-rounded human being, somebody as down to earth as you're ever likely to meet in his chosen profession. It also meant there was some natural outside skepticism that he was up to the scale of the task assigned to him.

The Sounders were in dire straits. Nothing less would have preempted the firing of a legend like Schmid. In the aftermath of that putrid performance in Kansas City, Seattle had just 14 games remaining to bridge that double-digit point gap. It was in that position for a reason.

The team looked disjointed from the opening kickoff of the campaign. The wound opened up by Martins's departure showed no signs of closing up anytime soon. The need for a playmaker was so obvious that it was an open topic of conversation in the locker room as the squad continued to struggle.

Lodeiro had just arrived, sure, but midseason acquisitions were notoriously tricky in MLS. The league's idiosyncratic style takes a while to adjust to. Even the best players often need a grace period of adjustment.

Otherwise, the Sounders looked like just about the worst thing a professional sports team can be: stuck between two eras, without a clear-cut vision for the future. For all of Lagerwey's talk about getting younger and leaner, the team still had more than a few expensive veterans on the roster. Worse, many of the hyped-up youngsters had struggled to impress when given the opportunity.

The conspiracy-minded part of the fan base suspected a rigged hand stacked against Schmetzer. The local boy done good was beloved among the most dedicated supporters. He had Hanauer's unequivocal backing, as had been proven time and time again over the years. That was no small thing — but Hanauer also took pains to make it clear that Lagerwey would head up the coaching search, and that the decision would ultimately be the general manager's.

Lagerwey hit all the right notes publicly about Schmetzer's connection to the community and how he was being given a genuine chance to win the job. Yet who but the most emotionally invested would have blamed the general manager for wanting to bring in his own guy? Having won the power struggle with Schmid, Lagerwey could strengthen his hand by bringing in a protégé of his own.

For the general manager, the situation was a win-win. On the off chance that Schmetzer somehow pulled it off and qualified for the postseason, then hey, bully for the club. If he fell short, the GM had an excuse to move on the hugely popular second-in-command and further put his own stamp on the organization.

You have three months to make a convincing case for your dream job, Brian. Oh, and you're stuck deep in a hole that's only minimally of your making. Good luck.

In some ways, Schmetzer's opportunity was a blessing and a curse: a long-awaited chance to prove himself, but one that would land both him and likely the rest of his coaching staff on the unemployment line unless they delivered.

Faced with such long odds and high stakes, Schmetzer and his staff refused to look ahead more than a week at a time. That's a standard cliché around sports, of course, but for them, it was something akin to a survival mechanism. They were so far behind, and needed so much outside help, that looking at the standings was both self-defeating and counterproductive.

Try as he might to keep his worlds separated, for a time, at least, the reality of what was at stake occasionally even bled over into his home life.

"It was so stressful," Kristine said. "I was so stressed. I wasn't nervous for the boys. I was just nervous for him. This was his opportunity. I don't know anything about soccer, but I do know that he's a really, really good coach. He's so self-deprecating, but I can say it. Talk to any of the players he's ever coached.

"I knew he could do the job. You just never know, at the end, if anybody else thinks that, or the people [in charge]. That's the frustrating thing. You do what you can, and then you have to let the chips fall as they may."

Had the rest of the season unfolded differently, the game at Orlando on August 7 would've been remembered for the incident in the hallway afterward, when Valdez nearly got into a fistfight with Eddie Johnson.

Valdez's scoring drought was into its sixth month at that point. It was fair to wonder how heinously he'd offended the soccer gods when, in the 80th minute at the Citrus Bowl, he received a pass inside the six-yard box in front of an open net, with Orlando's keeper out of position and nobody between Valdez and a gaping goalmouth. As if defying the laws of physics, he *still* somehow managed to miss, his shot angled sideways off the left post instead of forward into the net.

The Paraguayan was in a foul mood long before he heard through the grapevine that Johnson, his longtime social media provocateur who now lived in Central Florida, was attempting to enter the visiting locker room to check in on his former teammates. Valdez exploded into the hallway, shouting expletives at Johnson in Spanish, before he was dragged back inside against his will. Johnson just smiled, satisfied that his marks had hit so close to home. Truth be told, most of the Sounders found the humor in it as well.

The rest of the team was in high spirits. Looking back, most of them would single out that performance as the one that turned their campaign around.

Playing in muggy conditions that weren't quite as oppressive as the ones in Kansas City but close, Seattle could've easily wilted when Orlando took an early lead off of a corner kick. Instead, the Sounders hit back, and before long, they ran rampant. Dempsey netted a hat trick, two of which came off passes from Morris.

They defeated Real Salt Lake 2–1 the following weekend, then steamrolled rival Portland 3–1 in front of a raucous crowd of 53,302 at CenturyLink Field. In four games, the gap between them and the playoff spots had narrowed from 10 points to two — and Seattle held two games in hand over the Timbers, who occupied the sixth and final playoff qualifying place and were suddenly within close reach.

Just as promising, Schmetzer's new-look formation seemed to bring out the best in his charges. Lodeiro, alongside Dempsey and behind Morris, fit in more naturally than even the most optimistic might've hoped. Austrian winger Andreas Ivanschitz brought balance to the other side of the field. Alonso and Roldan, crucially, immediately clicked as the line of two defensive midfielders in Schmetzer's 4-2-3-1. With those two engaged, they could both protect the back line behind them and give the attackers freedom to create chances farther up the field.

For every player finding his footing, though, another was being edged out of the fold. With the team rolling — and this was a good problem to have, mind you — Schmetzer wasn't willing or able to rotate his starting XI as much as he otherwise might have. Other, less sensitive coaches wouldn't have much cared about the mental well-being of those further down the roster, but that had never been his way.

"It's like having 24 kids," Kristine said, "and you're only as happy as your least-favorite child. It's almost like the mom and dad relationship. He'll come in and say something about one of the boys and I'm like, 'He's trying very hard.'"

Schmetzer wasn't able to establish connections quite as deep as during the USL days, like the ones he had with Graham and Roger Levesque. That didn't mean he didn't try, or that the new reality was easy on him.

"We used to have them over for dinner," Kristine said. "Now, they want to go out with their friends. The other guys didn't make as much. A good meal was great for them. These guys can afford their own dinners now."

Some of the shifting dynamic had to do with finances, to be sure. As the salary structure ballooned, so, typically, did the swagger and sense of self-importance. Some of it, too, was out of necessity — if Schmetzer were to win over the respect of established internationals like Dempsey, Ivanschitz and Valdez, it was necessary to maintain a little bit of distance.

The coach felt as though he passed his first couple of major tests. The sit-down with Dempsey yielded the run of goals that had sparked the entire team.

A couple of weeks later, ahead of the away match at Portland at the end of the month, he won a staring contest with Roman Torres. The hulking Panamanian center back had been out for almost a year rehabilitating his torn ACL, and by that point, he was practically rabid with desire to return to action. The medical staff, though, had reservations about his making his first start back on Providence Park's turf field surface.

"Roman, we're going to be a little cautious with you," Schmetzer told him. "We're not starting you against Portland."

The news lit up Torres like a fuse. He puffed out his barrel chest, his bulging eyes looking like they were going to pop out of his head.

"I knew that was another critical moment for me, because I had to show strength," Schmetzer said. The coach didn't blink, and ultimately, Torres didn't begrudge him for making the tough call.

Schmetzer's dynamic with Valdez was more complicated, proof that even with all of his experience, he still had lessons to learn.

Schmetzer had actually been a finalist for MLS head coaching jobs before, first in Montreal and then with Dallas. In those moments, though he would've missed his hometown, he was eager to test himself at that level. Privately, even if he understood the decision to go with Schmid, part of his pride was still a little bruised that Hanauer hadn't trusted him with the Sounders gig from the jump. Only in retrospect did he come to appreciate that maybe he wasn't ready. Years of studying and second-guessing Schmid's decisions were a hugely helpful thought exercise once he earned the top job.

"At the time, I felt good having had success," Schmetzer said. "But if I'm honest, it was good for me to have that ramp up."

He was still capable of making missteps. Early on in his tenure, he promised all his senior players that every time he made a lineup change that adversely affected them, he would bring said player into his office to explain the coaches' rationale.

Tell them the truth, even when it's not what they want to hear.

Problem was, though he'd rotated Ivanschitz and Valdez on the wing for the first couple of games, once the team got into a groove, Schmetzer never fully told Valdez why he eventually got benched. Hence the moment, in early September, when he looked up from his desk and found himself face to face with a very unhappy Paraguayan.

"Look," said Valdez, who by this point had played in the top leagues in Germany and Spain and participated in a World Cup, "I've been with coaches that talk a lot. I've been with coaches that don't. It's no issue for me. But when you say that we're going to talk, we need to talk."

Schmetzer heard him out, realized that he had erred and apologized without hesitation.

"That was one of those moments when I realized that, when I say something to someone, especially a senior player, I'd better follow through," Schmetzer said.

Valdez accepted his apology, begrudgingly satisfied with his new coach's humility, if nothing else. Neither of them knew it yet, but the Paraguayan still had a major role to play in events yet to unfold.

It was subtle, but both men would later return to that conversation as an important one in the story of the season, when everything hung in the balance and hurt feelings could've dragged down the little bit of positive momentum they'd painstakingly built up.

NINE

My favorites of Seattle's old buildings are the crusty brick ones with tall windows, glass plates rising from wooden floors up toward rafters.

The weather here, as you might have heard, is notoriously gloomy. From October through mid-June, the sun appears only intermittently. Mostly, there is a constant gray haze, made worse by the early nightfall at such high latitude. The big windows, to me, are symbolic as silent protests to the conditions so often outside of them. More optimistically, they exist to soak up every fleeting ray, to take full advantage of each rare sunny day.

Consequently, walking around certain parts of Seattle in the evening is more voyeuristic than it is in most other cities. Those windows invite not only natural light but also attention. Every passersby can see right in — shops, apartments, restaurants — and get a sense for what was going on inside.

Writing about Clint Dempsey was an altogether opposite experience.

The grizzled veteran forward allowed as little outside light on his private life as he could manage. What was his was his alone — his motivations, his relationships with his teammates, his home life with his wife and kids. If an interviewer was perseverant, or caught Dempsey on the right day, he would crack the door to his inner sanctum, but only a little. Otherwise, he was inscrutable.

None of that is necessarily meant as criticism. In a lot of ways, his impulses were admirable. In a social media world in which so many athletes were obsessed with personal branding and image, there's a lot to be said for keeping the most precious parts tucked tightly to one's chest.

His reticence, however, sometimes made it difficult to convey the complete scope of a story as remarkable as any in the modern history of U.S. soccer. From modest beginnings in rural Texas, and having had to overcome a personal family tragedy, Dempsey had risen to the tippy top of the country's all-time goal-scoring charts.

Dempsey's private nature also made it challenging to get a read on his mind-set as he came to grips with the health crisis that cut short his 2016 season — and threatened both his career and, more seriously, his life.

In late August, in the aftermath of the home win over Portland in which he scored, the forward was diagnosed with an irregular heartbeat and sidelined indefinitely. Doctors were unsure whether he would ever play again. His face impassive, eyes as hooded as ever, it was hard to tell if Dempsey was worried or scared, both or neither.

The diagnosis was more noticeably traumatizing for his teammates, who were now forced to continue their unlikely playoff push without their biggest star and quiet leader.

Dempsey's most vivid early memory of the U.S. men's national team ironically came from the outside looking in.

The summer of the 2002 World Cup in Japan and South Korea, Dempsey had just finished up his freshman year at

Furman University. While contemporaries like Donovan and DaMarcus Beasley made names for themselves in front of a global audience — Donovan would be named best young player of the entire tournament — Dempsey still harbored doubts whether he could hack it even at the collegiate level.

Dempsey could still remember the lonesome sensation of watching the USMNT knock off Mexico in the round of 16, when the time difference between Furman's campus in South Carolina and South Asia meant he was the only one in his dormitory common room awake in time to catch the game. Donovan was just one year and five days Dempsey's senior, but in the twilight of that early morning, the gaps in their game felt yawning to the point of being unbridgeable.

"I was nowhere close to being with the national team at that time," Dempsey said. "I was just a fan like everybody else."

Compared with most of his peers, Dempsey was a late bloomer. Some of that was natural — youngsters develop on their own trajectories. Some of it was circumstantial, too, and that was the part that so burned in his core from the time he was old enough to grasp unfairness.

Donovan and Beasley were each selected as part of the inaugural residency program at the IMG Academy in Florida, meant to identify and incubate prospects from their midteens. While they played for the U.S. youth national teams and were fast-tracked to the senior squad, Dempsey was playing in predominantly Hispanic rec leagues against men twice his age and having to travel hundreds of miles round-trip if he wanted to find a more competitive game.

The tension between the guys who'd been given every advantage from early on and those forced to fight their way in from the edges was present even before that formative '02 World Cup run.

"That's where Clint and I relate," said Herculez Gomez, who also grew up off the beaten path in suburban Las Vegas and later played with Dempsey both with the USMNT and in Seattle. "We both grew up having to fight for everything — sometimes literally. He comes from a neighborhood where, just being white, he had to fight his way out of things. He still thinks about the doubters who doubted him from the first time he ever touched a soccer ball."

There was an undercurrent of tragedy to Dempsey's journey as well. He was imbued early on with an acute awareness of just how fleeting all this could be, and of the cost of his success.

He hadn't even been the brightest prospect in his own family. His older sister, Jennifer, was considered a rising tennis star, and the Dempseys were at one point forced to choose to support either her or Clint's dreams. They could only afford the time and money to regularly send one of them the six hours round-trip from their native Nacogdoches, Texas, to Dallas for lessons and matches. As the eldest, Jennifer earned that nod, and it was only after she died from a brain aneurysm at the age of 16 that Clint was able to rejoin his elite youth club in Dallas.

That painful arithmetic — on top of the already shocking nature of his sister's death — was seared into Dempsey's brain. Only through living up to his full potential could he meaningfully honor Jennifer's memory. Where others acted as though they had all the time in the world, or sought refuge in their own comfort zones, Dempsey had been keenly motivated to become his best self for as long as he could remember.

"I've always kind of been somebody who hasn't taken things for granted," Dempsey said. "I've always been racing against time."

That urge pushed him abroad after just three seasons in MLS, to Fulham of the English Premier League via what was then a record transfer fee for an American outfield player. Dempsey became a beloved figure at Craven Cottage, helping the club avoid relegation to the second division on multiple occasions. He scored what is probably the iconic goal in Fulham history, a back-post chip in a Europa League knockout-round match against Italian giant Juventus that led the team all the way to an unlikely final.

It wasn't just the goals but the way Dempsey scored them, and the swagger with which he carried himself. "He tries shit," are the immortal words of Bruce Arena, his former national team coach — as succinct a way as any to describe the attacker's style.

The chip against Juve was emblematic, the most famous in a long line of audacious shot attempts and back-heels through traffic. For Americans forever self-conscious about their place in the global hierarchy, Dempsey's fearlessness allowed them brief glimpses of a future in which they stood eye to eye with World Cup winners and didn't flinch.

Dempsey's exploits with the U.S. national team deserve their own paragraph. He was the only American to score in the 2006 World Cup, he scored the equalizing goal against England in '10, and he scored just 29 seconds into the '14 edition against Ghana — the first member of the USMNT to net goals in three different Cups.

His signing with Tottenham Hotspur in mid-2012 felt like a culmination of everything listed so far. Spurs might not have been Manchester United or Real Madrid, but the club undoubtedly existed in the game's upper echelon. Few Americans had ever approached such lofty heights.

By the following summer, at age 30 and finally at a big, respected club, all signs seemed to point to Dempsey's spending the foreseeable future doing exactly what he'd been doing for the better part of the preceding decade — bagging tons of goals in one of the most prestigious leagues in the world.

Behind the scenes, however, wheels were beginning to turn into motion that would lead to the most ambitious MLS move since the Beckham signing.

Hanauer originally thought Dempsey's purported interest in Seattle was a ruse; Roth immediately rang up Commissioner Garber and told him he'd do everything in his power to complete the signing.

The way the Sounders ownership group handled this particular piece of business said much not just about their own personalities but also about their visions for the future of the club. Hanauer was the practical-minded businessman, all cool rationality. He wasn't that far removed from the USL days — this was the guy who was still convinced the stadium would remain empty every time they opened up CenturyLink's gates on match day. Roth was the Hollywood producer, with a penchant for flash and sparkle. He hadn't invested in MLS, and in Seattle specifically, merely to survive. He wanted the league and the club to thrive.

Roth wasn't particularly shy about sharing his blunt opinions with the group: If Major League Soccer ever wanted to be anything other than the niche product it currently was, it needed to be more aggressive in acquiring top-level talent. He didn't just want to welcome in aging European has-beens, he wanted players near their primes, who could make a legitimate difference on the field.

He wanted, in other words, Clint Dempsey.

For a few years leading up to that point, in that middle ground between Seattle's successful launch and while it was still calibrating its long-term ambitions, Roth and Hanauer had discussed dream scenarios. Those almost always included Dempsey. For Roth, the Texan was the perfect leading man to put the club back on an upward trajectory. And so Hanauer, despite privately knowing the most likely answer, still reached out every so often to Dempsey's agent, Lyle Yorks, to gauge the player's temperature regarding a transfer back to MLS.

"No chance" was a regular refrain. Dempsey, with that motivational itch forever tickling at the back of his skull, still had fresh terrains left to conquer. By midsummer of 2013, though, that started to change. Having been edged out of the starting lineup at Spurs, yet content that he'd given it close to his best shot, the player was at least willing to entertain the idea of going home.

MLS was targeting big-name USMNTers with increasing boldness. The league offered an inverse of the prevailing narrative that sticking around domestically was a cop-out. Instead, it said, being the generation of players who helped soccer finally start to make it in the United States was a monumental box to check off all on its own. For a certain type of player who had tested himself abroad and satiated enough of his ambitions — and who stood to earn a significant pay raise stateside — that shifting narrative held appeal.

Dempsey would consider coming back to MLS, but only to Los Angeles, Toronto or Seattle. At that point, the league's bizarre all-for-one, questionably competitive single-entity structure began clicking into place.

Toronto ruled itself out, accepting that it was better for the league as a whole for such a major American player to end up in a U.S. city. L.A. was interested, but the optics would have been poor — the Galaxy had pulled in almost every big star since the Beckham days, and anxious to avoid the perception that it was a one-team league, MLS quietly shut that idea down. Portland was actually atop the allocation rankings at the time — and supposed to have first dibs on any incoming Designated Players — but all is apparently fair in a league run like a co-op, and it was told to step aside and support its biggest rival.

Hanauer was notified of Dempsey's interest and gradually convinced it was genuine. Roth got an email from Garber and went to work to get it done. The deal was by far the costliest and most audacious in the club's young history — at the time of publication, that statement still rang true. In sum, with the Sounders and the league offices splitting up the tab, the transfer fee and contract combined would cost more than $30 million.

Getting Dempsey to Seattle to complete the final paperwork was an ordeal all its own. In a testament to fans' fervor for the team, Sounders supporters began tracking flights out of London Heathrow and staking out Sea-Tac hoping for glimpses of the striker. One Seattleite posted a photo with Dempsey at San Francisco International, where he was connecting — though this threw the amateur sleuths off the scent, as Everton of the EPL was training in the Bay Area and some speculated he was there to sign with the Toffees.

When Dempsey finally landed in Washington State late that summer night, the club's brass rerouted him through a different door into terminal A and hustled him through a quiet section of baggage claim. A day later, via a contract signed in an upstairs office at Hanauer's house alongside Lake Washington, the deal was finally done.

Garber told *Sports Illustrated* that the Dempsey signing ranked "right near the top" of any the league had ever pulled off. "For the first time we have a world-renowned player who has international experience who's saying I want to come to Major League Soccer in my prime," Garber said to *SI*. "We hope that's the beginning of a new wave of players like Clint who will make the same statement. I do believe over time our business will grow to the point where you're going to see players like this in every market."

Garber's words would prove prescient, but the symbolism for the league as a whole was on the forefront of few Seattle minds on the afternoon of August 3, 2013, when Dempsey stepped out of the tunnel at halftime of a home match against Toronto wearing a gray hoodie. He walked out to midfield, flanked by Roth and Hanauer, and unzipped it, revealing a Rave Green jersey underneath.

Dempsey was a Sounder, and in many ways the personification of everything the club purported itself to be and hoped to one day accomplish.

"I think we were at a point when I felt like we were flat," Wright said of the mind-set of the organization at the time. "All of a sudden, we hit a plateau. I felt like we had an opportunity to fall off. And then: Dempsey. Dempsey changed all that. So much of it is relevancy and perspective. 'These guys are getting Clint Dempsey?!' Some skepticism with where the franchise was going to go changed as soon as Dempsey came in."

Dempsey didn't always live up to the hype surrounding his arrival. Given the overwrought symbolism baked into his prodigal-son-like return, that might have been impossible. His production struggled to justify an annual wage that topped out at nearly $6.7 million per year. Income inequality was so extreme in a league with such a paltry minimum salary that that probably *was* impossible.

He scored just once in 12 total appearances in the few months after he debuted, a campaign that ended with a humiliating series loss in Portland.

Dempsey didn't really embrace being the face of the franchise; he wasn't very often active within the community or to be found on local television commercials. The Sounders knew they were getting a notoriously reticent superstar; it still wouldn't have been a completely unfair criticism to knock the forward for showing such little interest in growing the game in the region.

Yet Dempsey still possessed skills that few in the history of the league could match, especially at his relatively young age. If he wasn't exceptional, he was very, very good throughout most of his tenure. His strike partnership with Martins, once it blossomed, was something to behold. Dempsey had always been something of a loner, both on and off the field.

"When Clint was coming up, the things that came easiest for him were still on his own," said Bob Bradley, another one of his former coaches with the USMNT. "But the best players know how to use their skills to play with others . . . to use their skills for them."

In Martins, Dempsey finally found a partner on a similar wavelength. Both players saw the game in similar ways. They were improvisational and would try to match each other trick for trick — "like little kids playing together on the playground," Dempsey once said of their chemistry.

In 2014, they were borderline unstoppable. Martins tallied 17 goals and 13 assists, finishing as runner-up for league MVP. Dempsey added 15 and 10, numbers none too shabby on their own. Both strikers took a step back in 2016, Martins hobbled by injury and Dempsey out of rhythm thanks to his midseason suspension, but expectations were high that they could regain their prior understanding in the new year. The Nigerian's shock departure thus affected his former partner more than just about anybody else on the roster.

There was something else.

Early in the year, Dempsey started to feel not completely like himself. He couldn't pinpoint the cause, but he knew his body, and something just felt *off*. His heart would flutter after routine workouts, sessions he'd gone through with no trouble thousands of times.

"It was just these morphological changes that happened to his heart," said Dave Tenney, Seattle's sports science director. "His stuff was not workload based. That was not affecting it. It was more just this unpredictable arrhythmia. There were definitely times where we could see that there was something funny going on, but we had no clue — and weren't in a position to diagnose it or see what was going on."

Few on the outside were aware that anything was amiss. He went through training every day, just like always. He was still scoring goals. In the weeks leading up to his moment of truth, Dempsey was playing as well as he had all year, invigorated by the addition of Nicolas Lodeiro.

Behind closed doors, though, Dempsey began sharing his concerns with some of his closer teammates. This had dragged on long enough to rule out any short-term fix. By now, it was obvious something serious was going on. After scoring three goals in the win at Orlando in early August and coming off as a second-half sub, Dempsey confided to Gomez that his heart was racing and that he couldn't get it to stop.

"Clint, you just scored a hat trick," Gomez told him at the Citrus Bowl that day. "Your heart is supposed to be beating fast."

Dempsey laughed it off, told his longtime buddy that he was right and turned his attention back to the game. That was his way — a peek behind a door that quickly slammed shut. Privately, though, the issue was such a concern that Dempsey had a chip implanted in his chest to constantly monitor his irregular heartbeat.

The issue came to a head later that month against Portland. Perhaps the scariest thing was that Dempsey himself hadn't noticed anything amiss. He actually played one of his best games of the season in the 2–1 victory, scoring a second-half goal and taunting the away fans with a throat slash gesture at the final whistle. The chip implant, according to Tenney, was what picked up an arrhythmia during the match.

"That's when he got shut down," Tenney said.

Dempsey was indefinitely sidelined a few days later and officially diagnosed with an irregular heartbeat by a team of cardiac specialists shortly after that. He underwent a procedure to correct the condition, and the team held out hope he could return for the playoff push. He returned to practice in mid-September, participating in light conditioning, and Lagerwey went as far as to say he was "cautiously optimistic" that the player could recover in time for the postseason.

But the repair didn't take. Dempsey went through a second procedure and was shut down for the rest of the year on September 27. Signs were positive that the issue was at long last fixed for good, but the experts thought that the first time, as well.

One more setback and most agreed that Dempsey would never play again.

When Dempsey spoke — at least to reporters — he rarely made eye contact. Perpetually rocking a five o'clock shadow, his hang-dog eyes fixed on some point out on the horizon and his voice monotone, he recited the same bland talking points he'd leaned on since his rookie season with the New England Revolution.

He simply liked to play the game, and no lone match was all that more important to him than any other. Skeptical of individual accolades, credit was always deflected back to his teammates. Don't ask about Landon Donovan, otherwise he'd retreat even further into his shell. At least in the latter stage of his career, Dempsey's primary motivation was hanging on for as long as he could in order to allow his young children to retain memories of his playing days that were as vivid as possible. It really wasn't any more complicated than that.

It was apparent, however, during the immediate aftermath of his diagnosis and throughout the long rehabilitation that followed, that the ordeal left a deep impression on him. How could it not? Every time he stepped onto the practice field, even if it was for only a few jogged laps, he was acutely aware that that time could be the last.

"There's always a little bit of doubt," he would admit later. "You never really know how it's going to go through the recovery process, not trying to overthink things. After coming back from one procedure and trying to do another one, there's always the possibility of that happening again. That was always in the back of your mind."

For those who had followed his exploits from a young age, there was cruelty in the timing of Dempsey's diagnosis.

He was just a few goals shy of matching and potentially surpassing Donovan as the USMNT's leading scorer, a mark he desperately craved even if he wouldn't publicly say as much. A fourth World Cup appearance, which would be a record for an American, beckoned.

With the Sounders on the upswing, he could finally make good on all the outsized hype that greeted his arrival.

For Dempsey, though, it wasn't really like that. Introspection wasn't really his thing. For him, the timing was a blessing: he had already achieved so much. If this was to be the end, he was at peace with all he'd done.

There were moments that stood out during the time frame — meetings with doctors, holding his breath as they discussed his options; the phone calls with Eddie Johnson, who'd had his own career cut short because of a heart condition. There wasn't really a single low point, however, an identifiable rock bottom.

"Not really, because I've had a good career," Dempsey said at uncharacteristic length. "I've been blessed with all the things I've done. I wasn't going to sit there and be too greedy. Obviously you want to go out on your own terms, but there was never a moment that was really, really low. Yeah, you're sad if your career is cut short, the goals that you wanted to accomplish that you didn't get the opportunity to do, but I had my family. I've been able to take care of them in a good way and play the game that I love for a long time."

For a while, Dempsey stayed away from Starfire, and by extension the team. He underwent his heart procedures on the East Coast and did the bulk of his rehab in those early months outside Seattle.

"It was tough to be around the game and not be able to play," Dempsey said.

As the Sounders' playoff push picked up momentum, however, and as his condition continued to improve, Dempsey was around more and more often. Schmetzer impressed upon him that his very presence lifted morale, and his star player obliged. He jogged around the ring of the field as his teammates practiced and watched home games with family in CenturyLink's luxury boxes.

Dempsey seemed to come and go at random, but it was obvious that when he was around, the group did perk up. As to how those appearances affected him personally, well, that much he never let on. Head down, one foot in front of the other, Dempsey pushed forward toward an uncertain future, his expression as ever betraying little.

TEN

Nicolas Lodeiro wasn't much of a talker. The Uruguayan chose his words, and his moments, carefully.

His English still needed work upon his arrival in Seattle, and he was quick to apologize when his message got mangled while bridging the language barrier. Even in his native tongue of Spanish, Lodeiro was a speak-softly-and-carry-a-big-stick type. A living cliché, he led by example.

The moment that won the respect of his new teammates, fittingly then, came not at the tail end of some big speech but from the silence that filled the Sounders locker room prior to his MLS debut against Los Angeles on July 31.

Lodeiro had made a favorable impression during his first few days in town. His reputation spoke for itself. As the play-making midfielder for the Uruguayan national team, he'd already appeared in two World Cups, including during La Celeste's stirring run to the semifinals in 2010. Lodeiro came to Seattle on the back of a prolonged stint in the Copa Libertadores, the prestigious South American continental championship, with Boca Juniors of the Argentine Primera.

His signing was lauded as a coup. Lagerwey spoke in barely restrained awe about what it said of MLS's recent growth that it could attract No. 10 from Boca, which was at the time still the leading club in the entire Western Hemisphere.

If there were obvious questions to be asked about the motivations of a player dropping down a level in competition in order to cash in on a pay raise, Lodeiro dispelled of them early. Where some might have eased into the fold after flying halfway across the world to start a new job, he practiced the very next day in order to prepare for that weekend's match against the Galaxy.

The focus with which he trained drew fawning praise from his peers and raised the level of those around him. They also spoke highly of his temperament, the lack of airs about a player who had already accomplished more than most of the rest of the roster could even dream about.

Still, locker room dynamics are a tricky beast.

Lodeiro was walking into a team stocked with established veterans and big personalities. Guys like Evans, Alonso and Scott had been there since the MLS expansion season — Scott predated even that — and such longevity lent credibility. Similar to Lagerwey's situation in the front office, even if the Sounders were currently in a bad place, the group had still never before missed the postseason and wasn't especially keen to shake up the status quo. And how would Lodeiro interact with Dempsey, Seattle's highest-paid and highest-profile player?

Consider the case of Neymar and Lodeiro's fellow Uruguayan Edinson Cavani at Paris Saint-Germain. Neymar moved to the French capital to escape Lionel Messi's long shadow at Barcelona, because the Brazilian superstar wanted to be on a team that considered him its unquestioned leader. Problem was, Cavani was a bona fide star in his own right, having netted 35 league goals in the year prior, and he wasn't all that open to being demoted to sidekick. Frustrations boiled over less than a month into Neymar's tenure, when the two of them childishly wrestled for the ball prior to a PSG penalty kick.

The issue went beyond the black and white of who got the ball in big moments. It was about respect and status. It was about whose presence held more weight inside the locker room — a crude and unscientific metric, maybe, but a legitimate phenomenon in the hypermasculine world of pro sports.

All that uncertainty still hovered over the Sounders as they prepared for that home game against the Galaxy, not only Lodeiro's debut but also Schmetzer's first as interim head coach. A nervous energy beyond the normal anticipatory jitters permeated the home locker room inside CenturyLink as the countdown clock on the far wall ticked toward zero.

Also understand just how important routines are for top-level athletes. They are creatures of habit. Frei, the goalkeeper, was so superstitious that he taped his ankles and fingers in the exact same order before every game, thumbs last — if he went out of line, he had to rip off all his previous work and start from scratch.

For as long as anybody could remember, floor-trembling pump-up music had been a pregame Sounders staple. The songs weren't always in the same order — or even from the same genre — but the background noise had been a familiar constant going all the way back to the franchise opener against the Red Bulls in 2009.

And so a stunned hush fell over the room after Lodeiro walked over to the stereo, flipped it off and calmly strode back over to his stall to tie his shoes. Sensing the puzzled faces and furrowing brows around him, he offered only a brief clarification: *We need to win this game, so we need to focus.*

"When he turned off the music, that was a moment the whole team witnessed," Roldan, the second-year midfielder, said. "You could tell he was serious and that he was committed to winning this thing and turning things around. There were, not stares, but definitely a couple of looks, like, 'What are you doing?'"

Those few seconds represented another pivot point. Whether Dempsey and the rest of Seattle's veterans ceded control or pulled the newcomer aside for a quick lesson in how we do things here would have a massive impact further down the line.

What happened to the humble, unassuming Nico from earlier in the week?

Who did this guy think he was?

If everybody is at least partially a product of their upbringing, few bore their roots quite as nakedly as Lodeiro. To understand him, the serene demeanor juxtaposed with the brash competitor, was to get a feel for the rich history of the Uruguayan national team itself.

The numbers do not compute. Uruguay, home to less than 3.5 million people as of the most recent census, is by some distance the smallest nation to have ever lifted a World Cup — and La Celeste had done so twice, in 1930 and 1950. It had also won the Copa America as South American champions a record 15 times, one more than neighbor and bitter rival Argentina and nearly double Brazil's tally of eight.

Wilson, the author behind the three-year rule, explained the discrepancy between modest population and outsized results by detailing the particularly Uruguayan trait of *garra*. Translated into English, *garra* means grit or guts, a national pride in success when the odds are most against their favor. Sounders midfielder and former Uruguayan international Alvaro Fernandez defined it as a willingness to die on the field for even the most unlikely of victories.

The most famous example is the 1950 World Cup final. For host Brazil, the tournament was supposed to represent the country's stepping out on a global stage. Brazil needed only a draw against little Uruguay to clinch the title, and triumph was so assured that an early edition of a Rio de Janeiro newspaper ran a headline describing their countrymen as world champions. Uruguay's captain bought every copy he could get his hands on, brought them back to his bathroom at the hotel and encouraged all his teammates to urinate on them. The underdogs won 2–1.

That, Wilson wrote, was *garra*. That was the soccer culture that so shaped Lodeiro's game as well as his outlook.

The modern personification of the term was Luis Suarez, who was equally famous for his goal-scoring exploits for FC Barcelona as he was for biting Italian defender Giorgio Chiellini during a group-stage match at the 2014 World Cup. This was somehow not Suarez's first biting incident; he sank his teeth into the forearm of Chelsea defender Branislav Ivanovic while playing for Liverpool in 2013. Nor was this his first World Cup controversy, having denied Ghana a spot in the 2010 semis with a blatant handball and shamelessly celebrating when La Celeste advanced on PKs.

Through all of this, Uruguayan support for their most polarizing son never wavered. When he arrived home in Montevideo following his expulsion from the World Cup for gnawing on Chiellini, he was greeted by a hero's welcome. *Garra*.

Lodeiro did not share Suarez's penchant for controversy, nor did he have quite the same level of talent. Yet it was possible to see similar strains in both of their games. Each hustled tirelessly. Tenney, the head of Seattle's sports science department, said Lodeiro racked up more high-speed running than any player on the field in almost every game, and that it wasn't particularly close.

Both of them had a penchant for coming through in the clutch — particularly for overturning games that once looked lost. Sporting director Chris Henderson liked telling the story of the scouting trip on which Lodeiro won him over. Boca was down a goal at home and playing lethargically, only for Lodeiro to almost single-handedly flip the result into a 2–1 win.

At his best, Lodeiro played with an almost palpable hunger. "That's my way," he explained. "I always play to win, and I like to prepare myself so I can better myself each day."

Lodeiro was close to Suarez off the field, as well, often paired with him as roommates while with the national team. It was Suarez, of all people, who helped translate a conversation between Lodeiro and Lagerwey when the general manager was still trying to persuade the player to come to Seattle earlier in the summer. In a country of just 3.4 million people, the world was smaller than you might think.

Lodeiro's arrival coincided with a wider demographic shift taking place throughout Major League Soccer.

The league still held onto a stubborn reputation as a retirement home for washed-up, mostly European vets, and not entirely without merit. The turn of the previous decade had brought a substantial influx of players whose Q ratings had long since surpassed what remained of their soccer skills. Some, like Thierry Henry and David Villa in New York, worked out favorably. Others, like Steven Gerrard and Frank Lampard, mostly languished.

Yet, as another part of the transition from MLS 2.0 to 3.0, Designated Player acquisition trends were also changing. Slowly but surely, the league's stars were getting younger and more impactful and tended to originate from a different part of the world. The league's collective wandering eye moved from east, Europe, to south, toward Central and South America.

Those in the know offered all sorts of explanations: South American top divisions played a similar physical style to that of MLS, helping ease the transition of new signees; investment in scouting had increased, meaning front offices could cast wider nets; clubs no longer required casual name recognition to sell out stadiums, so they prioritized signings that could win games rather than push jersey sales.

Really, the shift was all about economics. Players from Latin America, even those in their primes, typically cost less.

Increased quality of life also came up often. There was something greedy or unseemly in the way some general managers described leveraging aspirations for safety and stability in order to obtain cheaper transfer fees. The desire for a better life had become such a stock answer that it lost much of the emotional punch of what that actually entailed.

The story of Portland Timbers midfielder Diego Valeri was illustrative. Valeri grew up in Argentina, across the Rio de la Plata from Lodeiro's Uruguay, ensconced in a close-knit suburb of Buenos Aires. Valeri played for his neighborhood's pro team in the Argentine Primera for close to a decade, married the daughter of his father's best friend and had an adorable firecracker of a little girl named Connie.

Compared with most of his countrymen, Valeri had it all. Still, something nagged at him. He had grown up in a house, had fond memories of its spacious backyard. He wanted the same for his wife and daughter. Their suburb, though, had gotten increasingly dangerous. Apartment buildings, with their front gates and round-the-clock surveillance, at least offered the illusion of security. Not even that prevented the carjacking.

The Valeris had just parked outside of a friend's party in August of 2012 when four armed robbers surrounded their car. Acting quickly, Diego's wife, Florencia, scooped Connie up and dashed inside. Diego, not wanting to agitate the men further and worried they might storm the house, complied with their wishes.

With one gun at his throat and another sticking in his ribs, Valeri surrendered his phone, his clothes, the car, "everything." There was one hitch: the vehicle was a new model, a push-button start, and the carjackers couldn't figure out how to turn it on. Valeri coached them through stealing his own car, telling them where the button was and that they needed to press the brake to start the ignition.

"It's almost funny," Valeri said. "It's funny because nothing happened. But every day, things happen. People get killed. In that part of Lanus, if you ask 10 people, all 10 people would have gotten into this situation. Everybody. It's normal. It's almost funny. My cousin has gotten [robbed] four times."

After the incident, he instructed his agent to pursue a move abroad more aggressively. A few months later, the young family arrived in Portland.

"In every part of the world, things happen," Valeri said. "But you cannot imagine. If you are driving [in Buenos Aires] and you are stopped at a light, you need to have eight eyes. It's impossible. If you go to a park, you always look out for your phone and your backpack. When you live like that, it's really hard not to live in that way."

After his first week in Portland, Valeri noticed an internal shift, a gradual unclenching. He might never lower his defensive shields completely, but a few nights after they moved to Oregon for good, he slept more deeply than he had in years.

Valeri bought the house of his dreams, too, in a sleepy Portland suburb. The backyard was his kingdom: he imported the plush, green grass, had a pool dug out in the corner, painted the lines of his daughter's miniature soccer field himself.

"It's not about the material part," he explained. "I'll be honest with you, and this is what I've told her," he said, gesturing in his wife's direction. "For me, this house represents a dream come true. When we got married, or even when we were young, we would talk about how nice it would be to have a house, or to live in a neighborhood. And we couldn't do it in Argentina, sadly. Now, we can.

"You can see it in Connie, in the way she lives in the house. It's a dream for me to have a yard, and it's a dream because the way we grew up, economically, we didn't have the possibility to have the house that we want. I grew up in a house with a yard, but I didn't have a pool. I didn't have the possibility. That only means a little, but it's important."

Valeri was one of Lodeiro's first calls when he first began seriously considering Seattle's interest. The Argentine fielded these kinds of inquiries often. He'd become something of MLS's ambassador to Latin America. He, more than most, understood the concerns of potential newcomers, whether the league was as middling as its reputation outside North America, whether those promises of prosperity and stability were overblown.

He gave Lodeiro the same unequivocal recommendation he did everybody else: *yes, do it, don't even hesitate.* (Valeri's Portland employers might have later regretted their star player's endorsement.)

The idea had long germinated in Lodeiro's mind. His first image of the United States came via American cinema and grainy VHS footage of New York City's skyline. Years later, he was amazed by just how similar that city was to how he pictured it when he was a boy.

Though his journey was less dramatic than Valeri's and involved not a single firearm in the ribs, Lodeiro was motivated by a similar desire to provide for his family. His wife, Micaela, whom he'd dated since his teens and who grew up in similar circumstances in Uruguay, also wanted to seek out new horizons. Their first child, mop-headed little Leandro, had just turned one year old.

"I always wanted to come to the U.S.," Lodeiro said. "The effort from the [Sounders] was amazing. I have to give myself 100 percent for all of the work they did to get me here. For my family to be here in the U.S. is very important. I'm really happy to be here, and I think it was a really good decision on my part."

Though there was gratitude for the chance, and pride in providing for one's kin, it was mixed with an underlying sadness for those left behind. Lodeiro's "shoe phone" celebration, during which he took off a brightly colored cleat, pretended to punch numbers into the spikes and then held it up to his ear, quickly became a viral sensation in Seattle — but there was more depth to the gesture than met the eye.

Lodeiro's father, Alfonso, taught him the game, imparting love for the sport from father to son. Alfonso was the earliest and remained the lasting formative influence in Nicolas's life. He attended nearly every one of his son's youth soccer matches. As his career began to take off, however, Nicolas followed his dreams from his native Paysandú to the capital of Montevideo, a five-hour drive away. Following from afar, Alfonso would ply Nicolas for details after every game in phone calls that could last more than an hour, trying to piece together scenes in his mind.

"That's all we really had to connect us," Nicolas said.

When Alfonso died in 2011, the celebration mimicking those phone calls was his son's way of honoring his memory. After each important goal, Lodeiro lifted his shoe up to his ear, usually raising his eyes skyward for a few seconds before sprinting back upfield to join his teammates.

Lodeiro could still recall the exact phrasing of the advice his father would give him just before sending him out onto the field: "If you're going to play, you might as well have fun. And if you're going to have fun, you might as well win."

Garra. Even as appreciative as he was of his new life, a part of Lodeiro still remained in his homeland.

"Always," Lodeiro said. "I won't ever forget. I won't ever separate from those roots."

Back in the Sounders locker room the afternoon of the Galaxy match, the uncomfortable silence held for a few beats before the group released the tension with a collective shrug. *Sure, man, we'll try it your way.* The newcomer won the figurative staring contest.

Schmetzer, watching the scene unfold from the safe remove of the coaches' room, nodded his head and smiled. This he could work with. Veterans and young players alike were struck by just how quickly Lodeiro earned the respect of the group.

"You can appreciate somebody who says, 'Let's do this together,'" Roldan said. "It's a moment that strikes you and makes you think he's a leader from day one."

Most credited Lodeiro's unique blend of humility and pedigree. He could pull Morris and Roldan aside after training one day to pump up their confidence and, a few days later, grab the young striker by the arm in the tunnel at halftime of the Galaxy match to give him a gruff command of what he needed from him.

In any profession, hard work positively correlates with admiration. Schmetzer did not hesitate to make it widely known that Lodeiro and Fernandez had started coming into the team facility on their off days for extra reps. Lodeiro's teammates could not fail to notice how he headed straight to the gym at the team hotel to jog on the treadmill on the back end of cross-country flights.

"He was just super open from the very beginning," said Chad Marshall, the tenured center back. "You could tell he really wanted to be here. He cared. He bought in. His work rate, and his commitment to maintaining that level of fitness, is pretty remarkable."

Dempsey's health complications would not have been wished on him by anybody in the organization — and in truth, both he and Lodeiro meshed well in the four matches they played together before he went down — but they did settle the question of leadership. Without Dempsey, Lodeiro was the team's undisputed top dog.

It helped his cause that Lodeiro was so immediately impactful. Dig into internal motivations and sociology all you want, but the easiest way to win over any room is to perform at a high level right away.

Lodeiro destroyed long-held presumptions that any mid-season arrivals to MLS must suffer through an acclimation period. He dished out four assists in his first four matches with the Sounders, and four more in the first five games after Dempsey was ruled out for the year. Lodeiro added four goals, too, averaging nearly a point per game in 13 regular-season matches, being overwhelmingly voted MLS Newcomer of the Year over challengers who had had the full season to compile a resume.

His personality and sense of resolve rubbed off on the rest of the Sounders. So often impassive earlier in the year, suddenly every performance was infused with intensity. Sure, the do-or-die stakes were a motivating factor, but it wasn't as though the situation wasn't already dire when Lodeiro arrived.

He, more than most, wore his emotions on his sleeve. To watch him insatiably chase the ball deep inside his own half, kicking at an opponent's ankles, was to get a sense for the breadth of his story — the upbringing within a proud soccer culture, the death of his father, the opportunity America represented for his family that he didn't intend to waste.

There was nothing a Uruguayan loved more than a long shot. If these Sounders weren't exactly the famous 1950 La Celeste team, odds remained low that they would qualify for the postseason, let alone challenge for a championship.

If they were to do this for real, they would require more than a little bit of *garra*. Fortunately for all involved, Lodeiro had enough to go around.

ELEVEN

JORDAN MORRIS CLUTCHED ONTO the final few rungs of the ladder with clammy fists before begrudgingly pulling himself out the top of the escape hatch.

"I don't like heights," Morris murmured by way of explanation, as if that weren't immediately obvious.

His mother, Leslie, and older brothers Christopher and Julian surrounded him in a protective semicircle, backs to the precipice. Morris distracted himself by checking social media on Leslie's phone — his own battery had long since been drained to zero by incoming text messages and notifications of goodwill — and kept one hand on the wall of the Space Needle's spire for support.

The crow's nest above Seattle's most iconic architectural landmark was accessible only by a hidden staircase concealed within the saucer-like public observation deck. The nest was reserved for special occasions: for the raising of the 12th Man flag on days before Seahawks playoff games, for example, or for photo ops with the most anticipated rookie signing in Sounders history.

January 21, 2016, was a seminal day in Morris's young life. Having woken up the previous morning in Germany, the 21-year-old had flown halfway around the world, out of Frankfurt with a connection in San Francisco before finally landing at Sea-Tac. He agreed to terms with his hometown Sounders, putting pen to paper on the richest rookie contract in Major League Soccer history. And he had temporarily beaten back his fear of heights and made it all the way up the crow's nest, more than 500 feet above the buzzing city streets below.

Photographers coaxed him off the inner wall and toward the edge — *a little farther, a little farther, now smile* — hoping to line up the money shot with Seattle's skyline in the background. His hair slicked onto his forehead with rain and a Sounders scarf lifted gamely above his head, Morris tried his best to give them what they wanted.

He glanced over his shoulder just once, his all-American good looks giving way to a flash of sheer terror. In truth, the nest isn't as scary as it might sound. Even if one were to somehow topple over its protective railing, the roof of the observation deck a dozen or so feet below would catch you long before you reached sea level.

From Morris's vantage point, though, from where he stood, it was a long way down.

Morris grew up around the sport. His father, Michael, had been the Sounders' team doctor for years, going back to the club's minor-league days in the early 2000s. He'd attended games for as long as he could remember, first at dilapidated old Memorial Stadium at the needle's base and then at CenturyLink Field. The youngster was actually in the stands for that momentous MLS opener against the Red Bulls in 2009, a preteen full of far-fetched dreams.

Michael and Leslie were supportive of their children but not pushy. Jordan showed an aptitude for soccer early on in his youth in Mercer Island, a moneyed suburb on Seattle's east side. With a boyish enthusiasm for running in behind opposing defenses, Morris was good, but it wasn't as though he was immediately tabbed for future stardom. He stood out from most of his peers first at Eastside FC and later the Sounders academy, but what did that mean, really, in the grand scheme of things?

It wasn't until college coaches started sniffing around that the Morrises first began considering the sport as a vehicle for greater things. Jordan felt at home on his very first visit to Stanford University. Here was a campus full of strivers who were driven to become the best in their respective fields but who were well rounded enough to see the bigger picture.

He was a late bloomer, and though soccer was his preeminent passion, Morris always had interests and ambitions beyond the soccer field. That's partially why, when the Sounders tried to coax him into leaving school early after both his freshman and sophomore years once he'd developed into a star, Morris politely told them thanks, but no thanks.

He loved Palo Alto and his Cardinal teammates. He felt compelled to deliver the program's first Division I championship, which he would make good on as a junior en route to national player of the year honors. If the Sounders were that interested and invested in him after years one and two, surely the offer would still be there whenever he felt ready to make the leap. Problem was, at least from a Sounders perspective, by the time Morris finally decided to turn pro in late 2015, they were no longer his only suitors.

The jumping-off point of his rapid ascension could be dated to May 2014, when the USMNT used Stanford's facilities for training camp prior to that summer's World Cup in Brazil. U.S. coach Jurgen Klinsmann arranged for a closed-door scrimmage against the college kids to keep his guys sharp, much to the delight of the Cardinal.

"We were all so excited," Morris said. "It was the biggest game of our lives."

That last line would later be eclipsed, but it was certainly true at the time. And in what would become a running theme, Morris rose to the occasion. With Stanford mostly pinned back by its illustrious opponents, scoring chances were few and far between. When Morris finally shook free on the counterattack, though, he picked his shot with poise and splashed it into the back of the net.

It was a fleeting moment, a few seconds at most. But for whatever reason, it stuck with Klinsmann, and later that same year Morris was called into USMNT camp. In late September, he became the first collegiate player to make a national team appearance since 1999. In his first start against rival Mexico the following April, he scored the opening goal, pouncing on a deflected pass, shooting beneath an onrushing goalie and celebrating with a primal roar.

All the while, the hype machine was being ratcheted up. American soccer fans had been desperate for a breakout star for time immemorial — or, at the very least, since the country ended its four-decade World Cup drought in 1990 — and glommed themselves onto any precocious youngster who dared flash potentially transcendent talent (see: Adu, Freddy).

When it finally came time for Morris to make his big decision on where to begin his professional career, suddenly it no longer felt like his choice alone.

U.S. soccer in the middle of the 2010s remained uncertain about its place in the world. The USMNT had both improved drastically over the previous three and a half decades and struggled to make the final leap into a genuine quadrennial World Cup contender. The first and second half of that statement tended to cleave American soccer junkies into distinct camps — and Morris was caught in the crosshairs.

There were those who marveled at the sport's growth, at MLS's stability and the steady, upward trajectory. Recalling the spectacular implosion of the original NASL, this group was sensitive about perceptions of the domestic league. It lionized the national team stars who stuck around to help MLS grow, like Donovan, or those who came back from Europe to advance its cause, like Dempsey, Michael Bradley and Jozy Altidore in the wake of the 2014 World Cup.

The other camp was more impatient. As access to English Premier League and Spanish La Liga matches proliferated, the flaws in the American game were more readily apparent. This group took European superiority for granted, and rather than trying to lift MLS closer to that level, it would have much preferred that top American players test and improve themselves in some overseas crucible.

The two schools of thought were made manifest in the personal rivalry between Donovan and Dempsey, the two preeminent American field players of their generation.

Donovan played a leading role in two iconic national team breakthroughs — the 2002 run to the World Cup quarterfinals as well as the last-second goal he scored against Algeria in 2010 to secure advancement — and won a record six MLS Cups with the Earthquakes and Galaxy. He also flamed out with Bayer Leverkusen in Germany, later admitting he "took the easy road" in coming home, and had his achievements forever tinted by accusations that he couldn't hack it abroad.

Dempsey, meanwhile, had a less cinematic USMNT career but an impeccable club one. He was a regular in the EPL for the better part of a decade, for so long painstakingly edging his way up the ladder.

There was the issue of temperament, as well. Donovan spoke openly about his mental health and unapologetically about the toll of the grind, how he felt he was best positioned to succeed when cocooned deeply inside his comfort zone. He went as far as to take a leave of absence from the game at the height of his prime to recharge his psychological batteries in Cambodia. Dempsey, in contrast, was gruff and deeply protective of his private life. If he played with an obvious chip on his shoulder once he stepped onto the field, he wasn't especially eager to talk about how it got there afterward.

How one felt about Donovan's and Dempsey's respective legacies said as much about the individual's ideological and personal viewpoints than it did about what either man actually accomplished.

These weren't the subject only of barroom debates in soccer cities like Seattle and Portland or the hipster enclaves of Brooklyn and Berkeley. The U.S. Soccer Federation under president Sunil Gulati tied the well-being of MLS to that of the sport at large in the country to an agruably healthy degree. Klinsmann, despite being Gulati's pet hire, went the other way: the German had no qualms in butting heads with the domestic league, and if he never publicly stated he would rather the USMNT's best prospects blood themselves in Europe, neither did he discourage that perception.

Morris found himself straddling that emotionally charged fault line as he considered where to start his pro career.

Seattle's standing offer was widely known, but by the fall of his junior year, its interest was eclipsed by rumors linking Morris with clubs in some of the most prestigious leagues in the world. Sounders fans followed along with trepidation, having long assumed the hometown kid would someday be theirs; Europhiles implored him to break from Donovan's well-worn path and test himself against the best.

Try as he might, Morris struggled to tune out what he called, in showing off that Stanford education, "superfluous noise." He stopped checking his social media mentions halfway through the Cardinal's title run, overwhelmed by the attention and a bit discomfited with being turned into a talking point.

His decision was complicated by a January trial with Werder Bremen of the German Bundesliga — a tryout set up by Klinsmann himself, much to MLS's chagrin. Morris stayed away from Twitter throughout but found a different set of voices piping up outside the echo chamber's. A number of USMNT teammates reached out with advice. Yedlin, the former Sounder, could relate to a fellow Seattle native considering an overseas move, having transferred to Tottenham the year before. Morris remembered how content Altidore looked following his return to MLS from England, how much being close to family lifted his spirits.

Real Salt Lake goalkeeper Nick Rimando messaged Morris on social media toward the end of his stint with Bremen, and the gist of his message stuck: "It's up to you. It's your life. It's your journey."

Morris swore he gave Werder the benefit of the doubt, but part of him knew what he wanted even as he boarded his departure flight. He had been a Sounders fan since he was a little boy. In Seattle, he could ease into the rigors of professional life while looking forward to a home-cooked meal after training. Morris had some Donovan in him in that he realized that, at least at this stage of his career, he was likelier to thrive when backed by a strong support system rather than isolated many thousands of miles away.

Longtime U.S. national team midfielder Jermaine Jones would later mock Morris for making the decision based on being close to family, his girlfriend, his dog and "all that kind of stuff," but that critique was a bit ridiculous when one took half a step back. Perhaps professional athletes occupied a unique ecosystem, but in what walk of life were those types of considerations worthy of ridicule?

"Jordan had to live his life," said Donovan, who sent Morris a postdecision email expressing admiration for how he had handled the hoopla. "Everybody can have their opinions on what he should do and what he should be. He's the one who's living his life day to day. I want Jordan to succeed. I want him to be a superstar and help us win a World Cup just like everybody else. But more than that, I want Jordan to be happy and have a good life."

Said Morris, with more maturity than some of his much-older critics: "What I've realized is that you can be dehumanized a little bit. It's fair. People want success. But you have to look at players as humans, too. There's a life outside of soccer that's important. For me, coming back around my family was really important to me. If you're on the outside looking in, it's hard to see that sometimes."

If Morris took the easy road, it contained some sizable potholes as it wound through his first few weeks and months in Seattle. His decision made him an appealing punching bag for the faction of USMNT fans who had rooted for him to go abroad. Every heavy touch, each missed opportunity in front of the goal, was held up as proof that he'd made the wrong move.

His hometown club didn't do him many favors, either. At Morris's official unveiling, during which he sat flanked by Schmid, Lagerwey, Hanauer and Henderson, the front office talked a lot about the need to shield Morris from any undue pressure or expectation. Plenty of that was already being heaped onto his shoulders as it was.

"I was present in Washington, D.C., when they announced Freddy Adu," Lagerwey said. "And I refuse to make Jordan a pawn or a symbol."

A few hours later, the club's official Twitter account sent out the photo of Morris atop the Space Needle side by side with a similar shot of Lionel Messi from when the FC Barcelona superstar had visited the city. Because nothing plays down the hype with a direct comparison — even if tongue in cheek — with perhaps the greatest soccer player of all time. Billboards plastered with Morris's face arose around town.

Likewise, Schmid planned on limiting Morris's minutes in the early portion of his rookie year. By rotating four forwards through three starting spots, the coach would limit exposure and wear and tear for each of them. Once Martins headed to China, though, the Nigerian took those well-laid plans out the exit door with him. With Valdez slumping and Dempsey less effective without the rapport he'd established with Martins, Morris was suddenly expected to make up for the lost production.

Whether it was the share of the attacking load he was being asked to carry, the fact he hadn't had a meaningful break since the preceding summer or the residual stress of having to make such an important life decision — likely a combination of all three — Morris cracked beneath the strain.

Thrown immediately into the starting lineup, the young forward was held scoreless in his first five professional games. Shots went wide. Teammates would play him in alone on goal and Morris would freeze, hesitating long enough for opposing defenders to shove him off the ball.

Salt in an open wound, the under-23 U.S. national team he spearheaded lost to Colombia in an Olympic qualifying playoff that March, snuffing out what Morris described as a lifelong dream to play in the Games. Citing the psychological toll of so many setbacks coming so soon after one another, Schmid benched him for the home match against Montreal on April 2.

Playing on the wing, rather than at center forward as he'd done throughout most of his collegiate career, Morris looked bereft. Later, he would admit that his confidence sank so low he caught himself looking up at the ticking clock and wishing the games would just end.

"I was almost waiting for the whistle," Morris said. "I'm like: 'I'm too nervous to be out here. I don't know what's going on.'"

Like most of us, Morris claimed not to give too much credence to what other people thought about him. Also like most of us, deep down he did crave at least some measure of outside validation.

More than he'd have liked, he read like an open book. One could take stock of his self-confidence and mood on any given day with a quick observation of his body language. When Morris went through a scoring drought, it was as if a dark, cartoonish cloud hovered overhead. His shoulders slumped and his brow furrowed, his mouth contorted into a pained frown. On at least one memorable occasion, he laid on his stomach and pounded his fists into the soppy turf like an overgrown toddler.

"He's hard on himself," Seattle assistant Ante Razov said. "We've tried to work on his reactions. If the play doesn't come off, if you lose the ball, don't put your head down. We know you're upset. You don't have to apologize to anyone and show the world. Just get on with it."

Morris started to dread going to training, even more preparing for matches. He started playing nervously, tentatively, trying to avoid mistakes instead of making positive plays. Schmid could see the anguish on his young forward's face and finally called him into his office after an especially poor training session in early April.

"You're not having any fun out there," the old coach told him. "I haven't seen you smile on the field in a long time."

He was right, Morris realized. When Schmid implored him to stop torturing himself, reassuring that the coaching staff was going to stick with him no matter what, the tight little ball of anxiety in his abdomen began to uncoil. Finally scoring a goal helped, too. The dam broke on April 16 when he netted the game-winner against Philadelphia and ran toward the corner flag less in triumph more than relief.

From there, Morris scored in three more straight matches. He dribbled around two Colorado Rapids and finished inside the near post. He scored the game-winner against Columbus in the 88th minute and notched the clincher against San Jose a week later.

Mid-May, however, brought another disappointment. Despite his ongoing hot streak, Morris was left off the USMNT roster for the Copa América Centenario. The combined South, Central and North American championship was to be contested on U.S. soil for the first time, with Seattle one of the chosen host cities.

The verdict ultimately came down to Morris and 33-year-old Earthquakes forward Chris Wondolowski, Klinsmann revealed when the squad was released, a decision many American fans would've considered straightforward enough, given Morris's relative youth and big-game chops. If Klinsmann meant it as a rebuke to Morris for choosing Seattle after he went through the trouble of setting up the trial at Bremen, the German coach never fully admitted as much. Privately, Morris couldn't help but take it that way.

It had been a long year, and the calendar hadn't yet flipped past the midway point.

Up in the same stands that first encouraged the dream that would become a career, Morris rediscovered his passion, the competitive drive that could have either crushed him or been put to positive ends.

When the USMNT lucked into a Copa América quarter-final date with Ecuador at CenturyLink, of all places, few would have blamed Morris for keeping his distance. His parents' couch would've been a safer alternative to facing his bruised pride head on, racking his brain for all the reasons he was up in Section 122 instead of tearing it up down on the turf.

Yet Morris, alongside Sounders teammate, best friend and fellow national team hopeful Roldan, steered into the skid. A goofy, floppy Uncle Sam hat atop his head, he and Roldan led local fans in the traditional march to the stadium and stood with them in the boisterous North End.

The experience could have further dented Morris's fragile self-confidence, but instead it inspired him. From there on out, he played with an edge, fiery eyes burning behind that good-guy facade. Instead of pouting after every missed chance, more often than not he hopped back up, put his head down and sprinted back toward the fray.

"I thought there was a little shift in personality," Roldan said. "It drove him. He was bummed that he didn't make the [Copa América] team, and he wanted to show the nation he was capable of being there. I think he definitely showed that."

Morris agreed. "It added a little fuel to my fire to try to get back. The rest of the season, that was kind of in the back of my mind."

Morris scored in the 1–1 draw against Toronto on July 2 and again in the atypical romp of Dallas a week and a half later. Despite his close, personal relationship with Schmid — and at another potential inflection point that could've sent his season careening toward one extreme or the other — Morris came into his own in the weeks after Schmetzer took over.

The addition of Lodeiro was a godsend. Morris was immediately taken by the Uruguayan's poise and leadership. Lodeiro pulled Morris and Roldan aside after one of his first training sessions. They didn't discuss anything earth shattering, just their paths to this point and soccer in general, but the purpose of the gesture was obvious.

"He just kind of took us under his wing," Morris said. "He was going to be that leader that we could look up to."

Morris could recall with greater specificity Lodeiro's exact words at halftime of the Galaxy game, the first they ever played together: *Just run.*

"When I get the ball, run," Lodeiro said. "Just run, and I'll find you."

More often than not, Lodeiro lived up to his word, and their attacking partnership flourished. Lined up next to a rejuvenated Dempsey, Morris was dominant throughout the consequential 3–1 win in Orlando, dishing out two assists that could have been five, according to his veteran running mate.

"He's becoming a complete player," said Dempsey with uncharacteristic flattery, "not only somebody that can score goals but can get assists too."

For as promisingly as they combined during that few-week stretch, it was actually Dempsey's absence that nudged Morris over the final hump of becoming an influential pro.

"Obviously, when Clint went down with his heart problem, it was terrible and very scary," Morris said. "But I think it put more onus on me to be a little bit more of a leader, especially in being a scorer, putting that responsibility on me a little bit more. I love playing with that. I want to be the person who is responsible, one of those main guys going forward. When that happened, I put that on myself. That was a big change."

While most of his teammates still looked shell-shocked by the Dempsey news, Morris scored against Portland and again versus Vancouver. The rookie single-handedly took over the second half of the Galaxy match in Southern California in late September. Morris bent the game to his will, shouldering off opponents and showing off a newfound finishing touch, scoring twice in a 10-minute stretch to lock up a pivotal 4–2 victory.

It felt as though he had packed a decade of experiences into a nine-month span, but much to the astonishment even of those in his corner, the best was still yet to come.

TWELVE

As it turned out, the Sounders qualified for the postseason without much drama. That alone spoke volumes about the extremity of their midseason turnaround — or about the all-too-forgiving nature of the league's playoff structure, if you want to get all pessimistic about it.

Riding a high from Morris's heroics in the 4–2 triumph in Los Angeles in late September, Seattle then edged Chicago 1–0 at home and Vancouver 2–1 on the road. The 2–1 loss to FC Dallas was a short-term setback of long-term consequence — FCD playmaker Mauro Diaz, a driving force behind the top seed in the West, suffered a torn ACL in the match and was lost for the season. That would become important later on.

Technically, the Sounders were still playing for their lives into the final weekend of the season. A home loss to Salt Lake, combined with wins by Kansas City and Portland elsewhere, would've been enough to trip them up at the final hurdle. Nerves were settled early, the overcoming of a 10-point deficit as of late summer assured by the time most fans had even reached their seats. Fernandez scored for Seattle less than three minutes in, and though RSL equalized shortly afterward, Roldan sealed a 2–1 victory on the half-hour mark.

On their way off the field afterward, Lagerwey wrapped an arm around Schmetzer and relayed a long-awaited message into his ear: "You're my guy." A few weeks later, at yet another consequential Alliance Council business meeting, the club made it official, the *interim* tag removed from Schmetzer's title. The job was his; now he needed to go out and validate his bosses' collective confidence.

The Western Conference bracket was set. Dallas and Colorado, as the top two finishers, received byes straight into the conference semifinals. Third-seeded Los Angeles would host sixth-seeded Salt Lake, and No. 4 (!) Seattle would welcome No. 5 Sporting KC to CenturyLink. Playing at home, the Sounders liked their chances. In truth, they were fortunate their playoff run wasn't cut short after only 90 minutes.

If it would be slight hyperbole to say Kansas City dominated, Sporting was in full control of the rhythm of the game. SKC had been eliminated in shock fashion by eventual champion Portland in the same round a year before, when only a late game-tying goal and would-be-winning penalty kick bouncing off both posts and out denied the team's progression. That painful memory clearly spurred Kansas City forward. It was not intimidated either by the stakes or by Seattle's typically noisy home crowd. Benny Feilhaber was everywhere, spraying passes to all corners of the field from his place in Sporting's midfield.

CenturyLink Field was stunned into silence in the 53rd minute, when Kansas City defender Matt Besler headed a pinpoint Feilhaber free kick into the back of the net. Besler sprinted toward the corner flag to celebrate. Based on Seattle's tepid performance to that point, that very well could have been that.

But Besler pulled up, gesturing at the lineman in anger. The stadium turned its collective attention to the assistant referee, his flag raised for offside, disallowing the goal. The decision was vindicated by replay, but only just. Besler did edge ahead of the green-clad defenders a split second too early, but it was so close as to have basically been a judgment call. What would have been a 1–0 Sporting lead was wiped clean.

Kansas City's sense of unfairness was compounded in the 88th minute, when Valdez appeared to surge from an offside position in order to get a head to Jones's cross from the left side of the box.

By that point, the hard-luck Paraguayan's scoring drought stretched back for nearly a calendar year. If the problem with some incoming Designated Players was that they cared too little, Valdez's was that he cared too damn much. It was as if the drought was an affront to his manhood. He carried it as if it were a millstone around his neck. He felt snakebit, cursed by the soccer gods.

"Everybody who knows me, they know how hard for me this year was," Valdez said. "I tried every day to make the best of it. At some points, I thought there was something going on against me."

It would have been easy for peers to hold Valdez's lack of production against him. That $1.4 million annual salary, second highest on the team, was more money than most of them could ever dream of making. That was a significant chunk of change for a return of two goals in 34 MLS games heading into the 2016 postseason.

And yet he remained as popular a figure in the locker room as ever. If anything, he was more beloved because of the way he shouldered his burden. The lack of output clearly bothered him, but he didn't sulk, instead showing up with a smile daily in an attempt to rid himself of his curse through sheer willpower.

"He's just such a great example of a professional soccer player," said Morris, who as a forward knew something about the psychic toll of a scoring drought. "That stuff can weigh on you, and he didn't let it."

And so the rest of the Sounders looked just as jubilant as Valdez did when his glancing, diving header in the 88th minute of a scoreless game flew past Kansas City keeper Tim Melia and into the back of the net. Valdez's reaction said it all: he did a double take before popping off the turf to celebrate, his face looking as stunned as anybody's that one of his shots had finally found its way over the line.

At the final whistle a few minutes later, Valdez dropped to his knees, arms raised and tears streaming freely down his face.

"I've been feeling like there's been a big mountain on top of me all season," Valdez said, eyes still red-rimmed and watery half an hour after the match. "Finally, with the goal, that mountain went away and the pressure has been relieved."

Added Morris: "He deserved that goal more than anyone. When I saw it was him and saw it go in, I was so happy for him."

"I know there have been people out there who have said things," Schmetzer said afterward, in a not-too-veiled dig at Eddie Johnson, "and we get it. We're all pros. We understand the business we're in. But for him to come through in such a critical moment is well deserved. He carried the team on his back here, and I'm so happy for Nelson Valdez."

The Western Conference semifinal against top-seeded Dallas was more straightforward. The series was notable only for the barrage of three Sounders goals in less than eight minutes of the first leg — the first glimpse that even without Dempsey, this team had not only the persistence but also the guile to make a legitimate championship run.

Without the injured Diaz, FC Dallas looked a shell of itself. It had already won the Open Cup and the Supporters' Shield, just the second and third major trophies in 20 years of existence for one of MLS's originals. The team looked spent by the effort.

Seattle ran all over them, culminating in that staggering eight-minute sequence in the second half of Leg 1. Valdez scored his second goal in as many games, because of course he did. Jones, increasingly influential as the season had gone on, played in the cross, a sweeping, crescent-shaped arc from near the left sideline.

Five minutes later, Morris made a slaloming surge up the same side. Once in open space, his speed was a sight to behold, and there was no catching him. FCD's Matt Hedges was rocked back onto his heels, wary of letting Morris past him, and the young forward took advantage of his tentativeness. Morris turned Hedges inside out, pushing the ball past him toward the end line before turning it inward toward Lodeiro to tap into an exposed net.

Lodeiro applied the coup de grâce three minutes after that. Goal number three was almost shockingly easy, Dallas capitulating completely and effectively handing over the series. Frei gathered a tame effort near the top of his own penalty box, rolling the ball out for Jones to carry forward up the left wing. Head up, Jones caught sight of Lodeiro streaking behind the FCD back line. Jones's pass was inch-perfect, and the Uruguayan was off to the races. Lodeiro ran past everybody, and though he had teammates open in the middle, he did it himself, firing a shot inside the far post.

The celebration was cathartic, months and years of pent-up emotions released all at once. Lodeiro leaped over the advertising signboards and into the first row of the South End, being quickly enveloped in a group hug. The weather was miserable, the rain pouring down in sheets, but nobody seemed to mind. Sounders supporters had been waiting since 2009 for a night like this, their boys playing unburdened and to their full potential.

Seattle was Western Conference final bound. That in itself was not particularly novel. It had made it that far twice before, after all, in 2012 and 2014. The confidence and verve with which the squad was playing, though? That was new.

Morris wasn't the type to complain, but the long season had taken its toll.

He hadn't had a meaningful break in more than a year and a half, going straight from Stanford's national championship run to camp with Werder Bremen and then to his inaugural MLS preseason. The "rookie wall" is a real phenomenon, the point at which first-year players, having grown accustomed to the much-shorter collegiate season, start to break down physically.

Morris's back was sore, and he was dealing with tendinitis in his knees. On top of all that was the private burden Morris had lived with since he was nine years old: he had type 1 diabetes.

No one was really sure how the condition might affect his career longevity, if at all. For both Tenney and Chris Cornish, the head of the sports medicine team, dealing with a professional athlete with diabetes was a unique challenge. Nor did Morris have many role models. Both Jay Cutler, the former Chicago Bears quarterback, and Adam Morrison, the stand-out basketball player who had starred at Gonzaga University over in the east side of the state, had type 1 diabetes, but the list was short.

Morris didn't really concern himself with the long-term implications. To keep himself sane, he focused on the day to day. Living with diabetes requires constant vigilance, all the more so if your body is your livelihood. Every practice day followed the same routine: He would eat two pieces of peanut butter toast, enough to give him energy but not enough to risk having his blood sugar drop in the middle of training. He tested his insulin levels right before and immediately afterward.

Even with as well as he had been forced to know his body, and even being as cognizant as he was about eating right and getting enough rest, there were occasional episodes. Whether it was due to adrenaline or what, Morris actually suffered through high blood sugar during the upcoming MLS Cup final, feeling so physically ill at halftime that he nearly vomited.

"Sometimes when you're playing, subconsciously, you don't really feel it because you're so immersed in the game," Morris said. "You start to get a little bit more tired and stuff like that. I don't say this very often, but people don't realize how difficult it can be.

"On top of everything, on top of your performance on the field, on top of doing media stuff like this, all the other things you have going on in life, it's just another job that you kind of have to deal with. I never ask for sympathy. Diabetes has made me who I am today. It's just part of life. I'm lucky to be where I am, and there's so much worse that can happen. But at times, it can still be difficult."

He'd been through a lot, in other words, lived a full year, even before he came down with likely food poisoning two days before the second leg of the conference championship.

Seattle won Leg 1 2–1 at CenturyLink Field, goals courtesy of Morris and Lodeiro, but that away goal loomed large. The Rapids were notoriously risk-averse, packing numbers behind the ball and attacking only occasionally. This scoreline played into Colorado's hands: All it needed was a single goal at home in Commerce City and it could protect the lead. At that point, the aggregate tally would be 2–2, and the Rapids would advance because of the away-goals tiebreaker.

Morris had either food poisoning or the stomach flu. Practically, it didn't make much of a difference. The charter flight over the Cascades was miserable. The young forward tried to sleep but mostly just focused on controlling his own nausea, willing himself to stay out of the airplane bathroom. That night, less than 24 hours before kickoff, he wasn't so fortunate.

"I wasn't throwing up," Morris described. "It was more [out] the other end."

Dehydrated and feeling not himself, Morris was neverthe-less in the starting lineup when it was announced the following afternoon. He said he felt less affected on game day, but it didn't appear that way. Morris put his hands on his hips during stoppages in play, sucking wind into his chest. He lacked his usual energy off the ball, trudging up and down the sidelines when he'd normally be making probing runs in behind the opposing defense.

"There were times in the first half where he didn't look like the Jordan we all know and love," Schmetzer said.

That went for the majority of the Sounders. Whether it was due to the exhausting nature of playing at altitude nearly a mile above sea level, Colorado's gritty style or all the energy they'd expended in getting this far, they looked flustered. The Rapids outshot the visitors 11–1 in the opening half, getting ever closer to the goal that could decide the series.

The match wasn't easy on the eyes, but it was certainly compelling — less a soccer game than a battle of wills. Fans dared not leave their seats, fearing they'd miss the pivotal moment that would decide an MLS Cup berth.

It finally came in the 56th minute. Valdez, who played through a sore groin for 88 minutes, laid out for a loose ball and poked it into Morris's stride. The rookie clicked into gear, muscle memory trumping his various ailments, netting the biggest goal in Sounders history past onrushing goalkeeper Zac MacMath.

Morris didn't get to celebrate. MacMath's cleat had caught him flush on the thigh seconds after he'd fired off his shot, and he remained on the ground writhing in pain. His father, Michael, the team doctor, dug his fingers into his son's leg, checking for any potential ligament damage.

Jordan hobbled off, limping badly. Schmetzer pulled him aside and looked him in the eye, one local boy done good checking on the well-being of another. Morris never dropped his eyes, his message clear-cut.

I'm still going to play. He would make it all 90 minutes. He'd certainly overcome more in the past.

The lead held, 1–0 on the day and 3–1 on aggregate. Seattle was headed to the MLS Cup final for the first time in its history. The road there hadn't been easy, but for those involved, it felt all the more worthwhile for the toll it exacted.

THIRTEEN

THERE IS BETRAYAL THAT comes with physical injury, a sense that your body has let you down somehow. Even the least athletic of us can likely recall the first time they pulled a muscle or broke a bone. There was the initial pain, then the dawning realization that you might never be quite as whole as you once were.

That sensation is compounded for professional athletes, for two reasons. First, their bodies are their livelihoods.

"Our body is our vehicle," Evans said. "Some guys are obsessed with cars. They spend a lot of time figuring out how to make it run properly, and how to make it run tip-top. Those are their obsessions. Our obsession is soccer."

In the era of advanced sports analytics, the most disciplined Sounders had it down to a science. They monitored everything from how many calories they consumed in a day to how many hours they slept at night down to the minute. Particularly for the veterans who had been with Seattle for a while, the medical staff could tell them exactly how much energy they should exert during each week of training in order to reach peak performance. When even those best efforts failed, there was a feeling of some greater power forsaking them.

Second, their line of work is such that injuries are inevitable. No matter how conscientious they are, or how finely tuned their workout regimens, athletes pushing themselves to the physical brink for nine months out of every year are destined to break down occasionally — or have some opponent without as much regard for their personal well-being come in from the blindside with cleats up.

To stay sane, athletes put their faith in recovery time-tables. With hamstring injuries, for example, they know they are going to be back in action within two months at the very latest. Calf and quad tears typically require four to six weeks of rehabilitation, and that rehab is on a set schedule: walking during week one, light jogging for week two, etc. Even with longer-term setbacks, so long as you can give them a rough estimate of how long it is going to take to get back on the field, players can deal.

Stefan Frei's recovery from a broken fibula was fraught with much more complication than he ever could have imagined when he suffered the injury during a freak training incident in early 2012.

Back then, he was still a hotshot prospect with Toronto FC. Though the team stunk throughout most of his five seasons in Ontario, early on, Frei mostly improved. As gruesome as his leg injury was, he told himself it wouldn't lay him up for long. With the confidence of an early-20-something, he threw himself into his rehabilitation.

"I'm always a cup-half-full type of person," Frei said. "When my injury happened, it was, 'Water under the bridge. Let's go. What do we do?' I was the fittest I'd ever been in my life, because 24/7, I was in the gym."

Still, even for an optimist like Frei, there were moments of self-doubt. He had to relearn the most basic of tasks, like how to walk, and then without a severe limp. Checking off benchmarks on the calendar helped, but there were still low points.

"You know how things are supposed to be done, but your body is just not willing to do it," Frei said. "Then, it's, 'Can I not do it anymore or am I just not there yet?' It can be difficult. You can kill yourself over it, and think that, 'No, you just can't do it anymore.' And you'll never get out of that hole."

Little did he know that rock bottom was still a long way off.

While isolated from his teammates, Frei tirelessly worked himself back into game shape. By preseason of 2013, he felt as in shape and physically competent as he had in years. Then 44 minutes into his return to game action, midway through an exhibition match, he advanced to gather an opposing header. In the same moment, a rookie forward on the other team kicked at the ball with a high cleat, catching Frei flush in the face.

The impact shattered Frei's nose — as well as his psyche.

"That messed me up big time," said Frei, who needed surgery and was ruled out for at least another month, "because I'm a firm believer that you get out what you put in. You work your butt off for a year, and you expect to be rewarded."

A boot to the face is not what he had in mind. Frei was eventually cleared to return to action, but mentally, he was in a bad place. To protect his healing nose, he was forced to wear a bulky face guard that played tricks with his peripheral vision, and before long, he lost his job to his backup.

Frei's contract was up at the end of that season, exacerbating the pressure. He was so adrift that he eventually asked to meet with Toronto's sports psychologists to deal with the stress. Together, they came up with a solution: if he were ever to get back to the player — and the person — he once was, he needed a blank slate.

"A change in general was important for me," Frei said. "But more importantly, I needed a change to people who could build me up again from the inside."

That winter, he was traded to Seattle in exchange for only a conditional draft pick.

The goalkeeper, wrote Uruguayan poet Eduardo Galeano, is the sport's martyr.

"They say where he walks, the grass never grows," so said Galeano in his epic book *Soccer in Sun and Shadow*. "With a single slip-up, the goalie can ruin a match or lose a championship, and the fans suddenly forget all his feats and condemn him to eternal disgrace. Damnation will follow him to the end of his days."

That might have been a slightly melodramatic way of capturing Frei's mood throughout the first half of 2014, but it struck the right tone.

Labeled as damaged goods around MLS after being limited by injury in each of the preceding two seasons, Toronto's meager return in the trade spoke to just how far his stock had fallen. Despite Frei's being just 27 and only a few years removed from being considered one of the top goalkeeping prospects in the league, the Reds decided there wasn't much of a future there. More problematically, at that point in time, Frei tended to agree with them.

Frei described his confidence as somewhere "south of the gutter." And though he somehow won the Sounders' starting job out of training camp, watching him during that period was to watch 90-minute displays of just how mentally delicate even professional athletes can be. Frei very obviously stopped trusting his instincts. The easiest of saves were fraught with nerves.

The lowest point, the very nadir of the hole Frei described earlier, came in late May of that year, in the second half of a match at Vancouver, when a teammate smashed the ball blindly back toward his own net to break up a burgeoning Whitecaps attack.

Most keepers would have let the errant pass bounce over the end line at the expense only of an opposing corner kick. In more confident times, Frei would've too. Instead, in a frenzy, he loped off his goal line nearly all the way to the corner flag. Even there, more than 30 yards out of position, Frei still could have avoided calamity. He might have taken a controlling touch, or just knocked it over the sideline for a Whitecaps throw-in.

But no: Frei wheeled and booted the ball right back into the middle of the field — "like a dum-dum," he would later pronounce — directly to Vancouver's Gershon Koffie, who gratefully chipped it into an empty net. A look of mortification on Frei's face, he picked up the ball and impotently tossed it back toward the center circle. For a few agonizing seconds, it looked as though he would break down into tears.

The rest of the weekend, Frei hardly slept. He watched the play over and over in his mind as if on an internal loop. A feeling of dread settled in as he contemplated film study the subsequent Monday, when the error would be rehashed in painful detail in front of all his teammates.

"Goalkeepers always know when they messed up," Frei said. "There could be a guy scoring a world[-class goal], and you're still going to be self-critical and wonder what you could have done differently."

Sitting in the darkened meeting room that Monday, watching his gaffe again on the projector screen and waiting for the rebuke he was sure would follow, Frei cringed. Schmid turned around and caught Frei's eye, offering just two short sentences: *Don't sweat it. We got you.* With that moment of mercy, the restoration of Stefan Frei — which would culminate in glory in December of 2016 — began.

"I remember driving home from that meeting and having the biggest smile on my face," Frei said. "I showed up the next day for work all excited. That's how I improved from the inside."

Every goalkeeper finds a different outlet from the stresses of his chosen profession. The reality of the position is such that, without some kind of escape valve, it is too easy to get wrapped up inside their own heads, dwelling on failures long after the rest of the team have moved on.

Seattle goalkeeping coach Tom Dutra, who played professionally at the minor-league level, liked to get outdoors. A boundary pusher by nature, he had summited Washington State's towering Mount Rainier on multiple occasions.

Former Sounder Marcus Hahnemann, who held the unenviable record for most goals given up in an English Premier League match, recalled vividly how he handled the setback — if not the match itself, or anything, really, after about midnight. As soon as he arrived home from Reading's 7–4 loss at Portsmouth, Hahnemann barricaded himself inside his den with a bottle of whiskey for a marathon session of the video game *Halo* on the original Xbox.

"I deal with stuff differently than most people," Hahnemann said. "I did a whole bottle of Jim Beam that night, and that was that. That might not be the best advice for everybody. My wife didn't think it was that good an idea, but there was just no way I was going to be able to sleep. A lot of the guys I played with, they can remember every goal they scored. They remember who was on the bench for certain games, all that. I remember nothing. Nothing."

Frei's considerably healthier creative outlet had roots in his youth in Switzerland, during which he spent countless hours riding the train from his rural hometown of Altstätten to soccer practice with a prestigious youth club a few towns over. Overcome by adolescent boredom, Frei entertained himself by trying to decipher the graffiti art scrawled alongside the tracks, his olive-green eyes forever scanning for flashes of color.

Frei was inspired. In his free time, he started dabbling with his own designs — "on paper," he's quick to stress, "not on walls or anything like that." It was like a door to another world. The medium was so spiritually different from the act of goalkeeping, abstract spontaneity rather than rigid discipline.

"As a goalkeeper, if you make a mistake, nothing good comes from it. Ever," Frei said. "With art, if you make a mistake, it can turn into something beautiful."

He could spend hours on his tablet, working on a fresh design. His creative spark came to him at odd times. He would go months without doing anything artistic, getting lost in video games or some other hobby instead.

"Then all of a sudden, I'll be walking down the street and see something — whether it's a geometric shape or some kind of sign — that gets the creative spark going," he said, snapping his fingers for effect. "Before you know it, I'm sitting for 15 hours in front of a screen trying to put it together. I'm addicted to it, almost."

Frei admired the work of Kofie Augustine, whose pieces contain disorienting blends of shapes and angles, and the Polish artist Nawer, whose designs are closer to the street art the keeper was so taken with in his youth. You can see their influence in Frei's own sketches — as well as the lingering effects of his full-time craft. There are hints of that formative graffiti art, vivid colors with added flourishes here and there. But the work is stark and linear, too, playing around with depth and perception. Lines crisscross the screen, forming sharp angles.

Even at rest, it was obvious the goalkeeping side of his brain was never fully disengaged.

"I guess I'm kind of a perfectionist even when it comes to this," Frei admitted.

With similar meticulousness, Frei and Dutra pieced his game back together bit by bit starting in the summer of 2014.

On first glance, the goalkeeper and his coach appeared to be an odd couple. Dutra was outgoing and gregarious, Frei soft-spoken and bashful. If the coach was the life of just about every party he ever attended, the keeper was the type to seek out a corner and blend into the wallpaper.

Dutra was very much a product of the Puget Sound's proud soccer culture. Originally from the outskirts of Olympia, the state capital, he played for the A-League Sounders and previously coached at Pacific Lutheran University in Tacoma and St. Martin's in Lacey. Frei, in contrast, was something of a nomad, having never felt truly at home anywhere from the time his family left Altstätten to when he landed in Seattle.

Yet the two of them were kindred spirits, in thrall to a calling nobody outside of the goalposts could ever fully comprehend. Stumbling upon the two of them together, poring over film or talking technique, felt like intruding on a private conversation spoken in a language known only to them.

"Tommy is a crazy guy; he's a goalkeeper," Frei answered when trying to explain the level on which they connected, as if that said it all.

It was Dutra more than any other figure that resurrected Frei's career. Schmid might have given Frei the impression of unshakable confidence in him after the Vancouver match, but that was only because Dutra had so consistently advocated for Frei behind the scenes during that early shakiness. Dutra saw something in Frei that not even the player really recognized in himself at the time.

"He's so daring," Dutra said. "He's not afraid. He puts his body in places that [other players wouldn't risk]. Honestly, it's unbelievable how daring he is."

The coach saw how gifted Frei was on the training field, and how those skills could again translate to game action if only he could rebuild the keeper's fragile self-confidence. Dutra also knew that if the Sounders yanked the rug out from under Frei in the early months of 2014, they might shatter him for good.

"At the time, we had a good team," Dutra said. "We were

winning games 4–3 or 3–2. We were able to recover from some of those mistakes, so why replace him? We're winning games. Let him keep growing with the team."

The turning point, both men agreed, came in July, during another fateful U.S. Open Cup match against the Timbers. At last convinced the Sounders weren't going to lose faith in him after every slip-up, Frei played as though a weight had been lifted from his shoulders. Instead of overthinking things, the goalkeeper just reacted, flinging has body left and right. He made seven acrobatic saves against Portland that night, securing progression in a competition Seattle would go on to win.

The Sounders faded down the stretch, but the goalkeeper's form only ascended. If the rest of the team regressed in 2015, Frei regarded it as the finest campaign of his career to date.

He led the league in save percentage, finished second in total saves and boasted the lowest goals-against average in MLS. Just as impressive as the numbers were his shifts in demeanor. Frei stood up a little straighter and barked out commands to his teammates with authority, his increased confidence radiating outward to the rest of the Seattle defense. By the end of that year, he bore little resemblance to the timid husk that had arrived in the Northwest.

Some might have rested on their laurels, wiping their hands contentedly at a restoration job well done. Frei and Dutra, though, had only just begun. Their attention to detail was such that Frei started bringing out a GoPro camera to training sessions so they could critique his performances afterward. You think the practices themselves were tedious? Try filming it, editing it and combing over still frames to make sure your angles and hand positioning were exactly right.

On top of the standard team-wide film sessions every Monday, the keeper and his coach sat down together every Thursday to run back the previous match again in full. They took advantage of every technology they could find. In recent seasons, MLS had begun recording games with a wide lens that captured the whole field — think all-22 footage in the NFL — and Frei and Dutra used it to study his positioning even when the ball was well outside of his own box.

How was he positioned at the beginning of each opposing attack? Where were his feet? Was his stance too open or closed? Was he hugging the post or cheating too far away from it? Every week, the two of them would freeze the picture, rewind it a few seconds and pore over even the most inconsequential of moments.

"Making saves, what regular people are seeing, those are the easy things," Frei said. "You just react. All the work we put in here, I know it's going to come out on game day."

The little things were what separated the mediocre from the good and the good from the great. Those were the things that insulated Frei from the mistakes of his past and altered his trajectory as he came into his own. By 2016, he was rightly regarded as one of the very top goalkeepers in all of MLS.

Another tactic Frei used to prepare himself for matches was visualization. The night before games, in his mind's eye, he would picture everything from the bus ride to the stadium to his warm-up drills. His imagination was so vivid he could practically envision the spin on free kicks that existed only inside his own head.

It comforted him to turn over various scenarios in his mind before he was forced to confront them in reality, at game speed. So Seattle's visit to Toronto on July 2, 2016, Frei's first trip back to Ontario since the trade, threw him off on a number of levels.

BMO Field, you see, had undergone a drastic renovation in the two and a half years that Frei had been gone. An upper deck was added onto the east grandstand and a soaring roof lifted over the seated areas. Even the stadium's catacombs had been upgraded and given fresh coats of paint. Much had changed.

The walk to the opposing locker room tossed Frei off his equilibrium before he even began to confront the wide array of emotions that were churning around in his belly.

Toronto FC was the club that gave him his start. It's rare for a goalkeeper to go pro and get a shot to start right away, yet TFC threw him directly into the fray. The fans were enthusiastic, encouraging even as the franchise took years to finally put out a consistent winner, and Frei remembered them fondly.

Toronto was the city where he met his wife, at a Halloween party at which he was dressed as the Incredible Hulk and she came in street clothes fresh off a plane from a cross-country trip. A TFC teammate, done up as Captain America, gave her a hard time for not dressing up, but for some reason she gave Stefan a shot anyway. Toronto was where the couple adopted their pair of shar-peis, both of whom would later become something of a social media phenomenon in Seattle.

Yet there were still lingering hard feelings about the way it all ended. Toronto wrote him off, and that rejection still stung — though Frei insisted he saved his animus for a handful of key actors rather than sully memories of his whole TFC experience.

"It's where I started my career," Frei said. "I met my wife there. We still have a place there. It's where our two kids — our two dogs — joined us. There are so many good memories, we have so many friends that we still have there, that I did not want to convolute that positivity with some of the garbage that I felt."

All of it, the good and the bad, sloshed around in his gut from the moment Seattle's plane touched down at Pearson International Airport the day before the game. He tried to lean on his usual tricks, trusting his and Dutra's preparation, but he wasn't himself during the 1–1 draw that summer afternoon. He was more tentative, tendrils of his previous self-doubt creeping back in if only for 90 minutes. It was as if Toronto itself had summoned them back up.

Later, Frei would regard that road trip as a blessing: it allowed him a dry run before the MLS Cup.

Many months later, after Seattle's own eventful run through the Western Conference bracket, fate had drawn Frei's former employer on the other side of the line. TFC overcame Montreal on aggregate in a wild Eastern Conference final. That result meant that Toronto, not the Sounders, would host the title game, as would have been the case had the Impact gotten through.

It also meant that if Frei were to help deliver Seattle's first championship, he would need to overcome all those various emotions once more.

FOURTEEN

THE BUZZ AROUND TORONTO was real and palpable. Walking around the city in the week leading up to the 2016 MLS Cup final, there was a low hum of anticipatory anxiety. Riding around on public transportation, it was possible to overhear snippets of conversation discussing the Reds' chances, and how a championship might affect the club's standing in the local sports hierarchy.

The Maple Leafs stood head and shoulders above the rest. This was a hockey town, first and foremost — the sport's hall of fame sits right there downtown on the corner of Yonge and Wellington — forever consumed with the Leafs' Stanley Cup drought that was coming up on 50 years.

Below that, though, the rest of the teams within Canada's largest city fought for scraps of spotlight. For one week, at least, Toronto FC elbowed the NBA's Raptors, MLB's Blue Jays and the CFL's Argonauts aside and stepped to the fore. Segments on the club ran on an hourly loop on TSN's *SportsCentre*, and local news radio broke in with word that tickets to the match had officially sold out. The tenor of the coverage was important too: not patronizing but actual reporting, on injury statuses and how the chilly forecast could impact playing conditions.

Now, complete irrelevance within the host city ahead of a championship game was something of a low bar to clear, but that was where MLS stood in 2016. It was still jarring to catch instances of such casual interest outside of the soccer bubble. Perhaps in no other major North American city with multiple other top-level professional teams would the match have been treated with such legitimacy.

The matchup, then, was apropos on multiple levels. Up until that point in the league's history, no two clubs had done as much to break into mainstream consciousness than TFC and the Sounders. Toronto sketched out the blueprint that Seattle added its own flourishes to, and MLS had risen on a steady upward trajectory ever since.

Now here they were, going head to head, each seeking to validate their own respective grand projects with what would be either's first MLS Cup title.

Toronto entered the week as distinct and deserved favorites. It went beyond home-field advantage, although that certainly helped. Whereas the Sounders had done just enough to edge their way out of their side of the bracket, TFC won the East in style. Its conference final series against rival Montreal would be remembered for years as one of the most exciting in league history — 7–5 on aggregate, the last two goals coming in extra time.

The Reds were led by Sebastian Giovinco, the 2015 MLS MVP and one of the most talented players to ever call the league home. His addition from Juventus was as much of a game-changer as Dempsey's move to Seattle had been a few years earlier. Giovinco was just 27 years old when he signed in early 2015, very much within the prime of his career, and he backed up his pedigree from the moment he landed in Ontario. He was in good form, as well, having tallied four goals and four assists in five playoff games ahead of the final.

Nor was Toronto a one-man team. Michael Bradley and Jozy Altidore were part of that wave of U.S. men's national teamers who returned to MLS after the 2014 World Cup, and each was hugely impactful on this day. With the league's highest payroll, the supporting cast was talented and experienced.

Looking at all that alone, TFC had the edge. And that was before digging into what few on the ground realized to its full extent at the time: the Sounders were gassed. Had they been given a glimpse beyond closed locker room doors, the Toronto faithful would have been even more confident of their team's chances than they already were.

The Sounders expended so much energy even in making it to the final. The situation was so dire when Schmetzer took over for Schmid that he'd needed to burn through every trick in his book. With each point so precious, there was no squad rotation, no games off for veterans badly in need of rest. As a result, even before they landed in Toronto, the group was battered to a point of near exhaustion.

Injuries had piled up. Alonso would require eight painkilling injections in his sprained left knee, four before the match and four more at halftime, in order to play. (Schmetzer was exaggerating when he said in the buildup that Alonso would "cut off his right arm so his left knee could play," though not by much.) Both center backs, Torres and Marshall, were at less than 100 percent. Morris was still feeling that collision with MacMath in the second leg of the conference final. Ivanschitz and Valdez were each hobbled by various ailments.

"We drove those players as far as they could go," said Ante Razov, the assistant coach. "I think if there had been one more game [after the final], Seattle would have lost 5–0. They had nothing left. We had guys injured all over the field. They probably shouldn't have been thrown out there. But it was a championship."

And so the coaching staff went about piecing together a game plan that might not have made for beautiful soccer but would at least give their squad a fighting chance. The Sounders would pack numbers behind the ball and allow Toronto to control possession. They would bend but not break, attacking only when they saw a gaping opening for a counter. They just needed not to concede — at 0–0, the worst-case scenario was a penalty-kick shootout and, hey, if they made it that far, they would take their shot.

All week the coaches drilled that mentality into their charges. *Defend every scrap of turf. Don't give in. At all costs, do not let them breach our defenses.* Best the staff could tell, the players bought in. Publicly, during press conferences and scrums in front of media assembled from all over the continent, Schmetzer radiated sunny confidence about his team's chances. Privately, he was less sure.

Athletes have varying strategies for whiling away downtime — and with the match not set to kick off until 7:30 p.m. Eastern Standard Time, the Sounders had no shortage of it to kill on the Saturday of the game. Inside their respective rooms at the Delta Hotel in downtown Toronto, they spent hours attempting to concentrate on anything but the nerves.

Every roommate pairing had its own rhythms: Evans liked to binge-watch Netflix or Amazon Video, while Marshall napped in the other bed; Scott and Erik Friberg mostly kept to themselves in their room, focused on the task at hand; Morris and Roldan, reunited once more after the stomach flu issue in Colorado, chatted excitedly about how cool all of this was.

Frei's day got off to an inauspicious start. He had enough going on in his headspace even before a panicky, early-morning phone call disturbed his slumber. His mother, Marlies, was stuck at San Francisco International Airport, being prevented from boarding her Toronto-bound flight over a visa issue. As a Swiss citizen, she had forgotten to file the correct paperwork on time, but surely her son the star goalkeeper could find her a way onto the flight.

"She was pretty angry," Frei said, chuckling at the memory. "Mom can get a little crazy."

You deal with it, he told his brother, Michael. *I've got a game in a few hours.*

Stefan rolled over and tried to fall back asleep, but to no avail. He couldn't stop the picture show from streaming on a loop inside his own head. Closing his eyes more tightly, he attempted to focus on the positive, visualizing what it would feel like to grasp the silver trophy with gloved hands.

Little did he know.

You convince yourself you can handle winter weather until you stand on the shores of Lake Ontario at night with a December wind blowing in off the water. Ask anyone who was there for the first word that comes to mind about the 2016 MLS Cup final, and the response is almost unanimous: *cold.*

Temperatures were technically in the mid-20s, Fahrenheit, at kickoff, but that didn't factor in the constant, whipping, bone-chilling damned wind. The late start time didn't help matters; the sun had long since set, allowing a deep chill to settle in. Heat lamps were installed at intervals in the BMO concourses, drawing huddled masses during both the pregame and halftime.

With space in the press and luxury boxes limited, some reporters were forced into makeshift tents off to the side, typing deadline stories through thick gloves. Players' wives and kids weren't given preferential treatment, either: they were sprinkled throughout the stands wherever there was room, shivering alongside everybody else.

"I literally had three down coats on," Kristine Schmetzer said. "I looked like the Michelin Man. I don't want to say this, but at one point it was just like, let it end, because everybody was so cold."

The players on the bench at least had a heater nearby, not that it helped all that much.

"It almost made things worse, because it felt like it was blowing out cold air," Seattle defender Tony Alfaro said. "You felt like you were being poked with little needles all over your face and body. It was too cold."

Prior to the pregame warm-up and in accordance with MLS rules, BMO's grounds crew sprayed the pitch with water, which had the unfortunate consequence of freezing as soon as it hit the grass. The ball picked up ice off the surface as it rolled, giving goalkeepers the impression they were getting peppered with giant snowballs.

"His warm-up was terrible," Dutra said of Frei. "It was like he was catching an ice cube. He's looking at his gloves, and I didn't even know what to say to him."

Stay with it. Just stay with it.

Frei struggled to maintain focus. The conditions were one thing; the taunts coming out of the beer garden behind the goal were another. Though they try their hardest not to ever show it, eyes straight ahead and bodies unflinching, athletes really do hear most of the barbs thrown at them by the crowd. For Frei, these ones were especially hurtful. Inwardly, he steamed: hadn't he played here for half a decade, giving these fans his all? Where was their gratitude, their sense of loyalty?

"I heard fans behind me yelling stupid stuff, then I turned around, and they were all really young fans," Frei said. "It made me feel disconnected, which was a good thing. This is a new generation. They're just fans, and I'm just the away goalkeeper."

Later, he would recall those insults as part of what allowed him to overlook the frigid temperatures and lock in. Later, some of those fans would surely come to regret the part they played in the action to come.

"They were trying to dig stuff up — 'I know where your wife Jennifer lives' and stuff like that — but it almost made me feel good," Frei said. "Feelings would have been stranger if someone behind the goal had been yelling, 'Stefan, we miss you. You're still the best.' It helped me get ready to go."

Few sensations in sport can match the final countdown before a big game. Anything is still possible. The anticipation is almost unbearable at that point, tens of thousands edging forward in their seats and ready to burst. *Please, for the love of God, just get on with it already.*

The pregame spectacle at BMO Field befitted the occasion. Red and green fireworks pierced the night sky, and both the home and traveling fans unveiled tifos in support of their squads. Most stirring of all was "O Canada," sung a cappella by the crowd, every bellowed word resonant with emotion.

"The national anthem was epic," Roldan said. "It was pretty emotional, even as an American. I was freezing cold, ready to play, with the goosebumps down my neck. I couldn't believe what kind of atmosphere I was in."

Finally, kickoff. Just ten and a half months after they reported to training camp — with Martins still on the roster and Schmid still the coach; how had it been only ten and a half months? — all of that work would culminate in a few fateful hours.

Toronto wasted very little time in establishing the upper hand. Less than two minutes into the match, Altidore chested the ball down for Giovinco, ran onto the return pass and bounced a shot toward the back post. Frei, slightly out of position, was beaten, springing helplessly toward his left. The ball rolled inches wide of the goal. Then 13 minutes later, Jonathan Osorio shook free in the middle of the penalty box but angled his shot directly into Frei's arms.

Otherwise, there were few flashpoints. Seattle defended in a disciplined block, with Toronto picking only at the edges. Roldan and Alonso stood firm in front of the back line. Torres and Marshall gobbled up anything that managed to sneak past the defensive midfielders, throwing their big bodies in front of attackers as human shields.

At halftime, Schmetzer was collected confidence personified. His game plan was working. If his troops hadn't managed to get much going, attack-wise, neither had the hosts been able to meaningfully threaten them.

Giovinco finally wiggled into an opening three minutes into the second half, with Marshall out of position to his left and Frei alone in front of an exposed net. The Italian fired into the side netting, and the moment passed. The clock ticked upward, slowly at first and then in great bounds.

Toronto could have won it in the 93rd minute, when a corner kick bounced toward Altidore on the doorstep, only for Frei to punch the ball out of danger with a flailing dive. Those two protagonists, Altidore and Frei, had been testing one another from the early stages of the game. Their pivotal encounter was still to come.

The Sounders had yet to manage a single shot on goal — they wouldn't, becoming the first team in MLS Cup history to make it through an entire game without such a tally — but it hadn't mattered. Their defense stood firm.

The whistle blew, signaling the end of regulation. Two 15-minute periods of extra time remained, with the possibility of penalties lingering on the other side.

A goalkeeper's life's work could be defined by a single moment. There was cruelty in that reality: hours and years and decades of dedicated practice crystalized in a millisecond of raw instinct.

Careers had been ruined, reputations tarnished, by a fleeting misstep.

There could be beauty in it, as well, as Frei found out in the 108th minute of a scoreless draw on a cold night in Toronto. For as long as he plays, he'll likely be remembered first and foremost for the sequence that followed Tosaint Ricketts's burst up the right flank past a lunging, heavy-legged Torres.

Ricketts floated a chipped cross toward an onrushing Altidore, who arched his back like a leaping salmon to get just the right amount of loft on his goal-bound header. Sidestepping from left to right, Frei gathered himself before backpedaling furiously, his eyes tracking the trajectory of the ball. The goalkeeper threw himself backward, reached the shot with desperate fingertips and somehow clawed it wide of the post with a flick of his left wrist.

Altidore, who was already turning toward the corner flag to celebrate and later admitted he thought Frei had no chance of getting there, put his hands atop his head in shock. That gesture was mimicked around BMO Field. The iconic photo of Frei's save by Lindsay Wasson of the *Seattle Times* captured the full range of emotions — behind the sprawling keeper, the same fans who taunted him before the game have their mouths open, some in premature celebration and some in shock.

"The best save I've ever seen in person," said Marshall, who had a close-range view from the middle of the penalty box. "One hell of a save," Altidore said in a tip of his metaphorical cap, and "One of the best saves I've ever seen in a final," in the words of Dutra. Frei was characteristically modest: "Sometimes you surprise yourself with the shots you can actually get to."

Whatever the exact characterization, Frei's moment of glory changed the course of the game. Beforehand, Seattle was holding on for dear life, an emboldened Toronto pushing forward around tired legs. With a flick of his wrist, Frei cast a spell of self-doubt over the stadium. Red-clad shoulders slumped all over the field, as if they realized all at once that this might just be one of those nights.

On the Sounders sideline, Schmetzer allowed himself to consider for the first time since he assumed the job whether this might just be a team of destiny, after all.

Penalty-kick shootouts are imperfect ways to decide championships. So different from the standard run of play, the tiebreaker can feel random, destinies decided by a coin flip. That sense of injustice was especially strong, as in the case of the 2016 MLS Cup final, when one side had so dominated the preceding 120 minutes of game action but failed to break through where it mattered most.

All that said, as human dramas go, PKs are as captivating and agonizing as it gets.

Up in the stands, Kristine Schmetzer narrated proceedings for Dutra's wife, Molly, who refused to watch and turned her back on the action unfolding below. Hanauer had been hustled down to field level for a trophy celebration that might never come, and within sight line of the players, he tried valiantly to conceal both his nerves and how freezing it was.

"I didn't want to be the guy they looked at who was shivering and then have them realize how cold it was," Hanauer said. "I tried to act like I could actually feel my feet."

In retrospect, Seattle's victory felt inevitable from the moment Frei pawed aside Altidore's header. In reality, there were still pivot points on which the whole narrative could've turned, alternative timelines on which TFC ultimately triumphed in front of its home fans.

The first round of any shootout is crucial. There's a reason coaches often opt to send out their most trusted spot-kick takers right away: it sets the tone for everything else that follows. So after Altidore finally got the better of Frei to give TFC the

1–0 lead, the pressure on Evans was immense. The longtime captain had come on only 12 minutes earlier with this exact scenario in mind. He hadn't seen regular action in months, but still Schmetzer trusted that he'd keep his nerve — and Evans delivered, rolling a low shot just inside the right-hand post.

Bradley had been great all night for TFC, but his spot kick was weak, and Frei easily blocked it to his left. Ivanschitz then caught Clint Irwin guessing the wrong way to stake Seattle to a 2–1 lead. Round three brought it back level: Benoit Cheyrou made; Alvaro Fernandez missed.

On and on it went, the stakes growing more interminable with each passing round. Will Johnson converted for TFC. As if in defiance of the pressure, Jones coolly smashed his chance into the underside of the roof of the net. Drew Moor returned serve for Toronto. Lodeiro, knowing a miss would have given the Reds the title, also found the upper corner.

In sudden death, the hosts finally blinked. Justin Morrow's shot hit the underside of the crossbar and caromed out. Seattle would have a chance to win it.

Torres often joked with his coaches and teammates that prior to a teenage growth spurt, he'd actually played forward back in his native Panama City. Mostly, they laughed him off — it was hard to envision him as anything other than the wide-bodied center back he'd become. Yet prior to the conference final, when they lined up to practice PKs for the first time, Torres stroked all of his into the corners of the net. And with the championship on the line, it was him that Schmetzer nodded toward.

Torres did not hesitate, striding confidently to the spot, splashing a shot into the back of the net and wheeling away with a bellowing roar that would become synonymous with Seattle's first-ever MLS championship.

The visiting locker room at BMO Field was a madhouse. Plastic casing had been draped over the individual stalls to protect personal belongings from champagne spray, not all that effectively. The players danced in the middle of the room in a sweaty, sticky, heaving mass, the big-eared MLS Cup trophy passing overhead from hand to hand.

Gomez, who had previously won titles in MLS and in Mexico, bragged about no longer needing goggles to protect his eyes from the bursts of celebratory booze. Morris and Marshall both noted that Heineken stings when it gets onto brush-burned knees and elbows, a revelation precious few are fortunate enough to make. The players broke into a spontaneous chant of "dou-ble bon-us-es" — clap, clap, clapclapclap — when Hanauer took his turn drinking out of the Cup, to much merriment.

Away from the mayhem, Schmetzer took solace in the back corner of the tiny coaches' room to reflect on the greater meaning of the achievement.

He hadn't had much time to consider the implications of the journey, having thrown himself into the weeds of it from the morning he took over from Schmid. Only now, with a cracked can of Stella Artois in his hand and surrounded by empty pizza boxes, would he dare articulate what it meant to become the first team in Seattle soccer history to win a top-flight title.

"I'm happy for everyone in this organization, from '09 and the guys that were there: Ozzie, Brad, Zach," Schmetzer said. "For the new guys that have been here, for the young guys that have busted their balls every day at training. I'm happy for them. I'm happy for guys like Alan [Hinton] who have such a long history with the club. Adrian and Joe, it's great for them, the money that they put into the club to start this. For my staff . . . I love these guys."

Here, his voice began to crack, and his blue eyes began to

tear up behind his glasses: "It's just so, so great. The most pride I feel is for the players and for the fans."

It was well after midnight when the players left the stadium, having finally showered, changed and gone through their requisite media responsibilities. Most zonked out on the bus ride back to the hotel, before another jolt of adrenaline: traveling Sounders fans packed the lobby, patiently awaiting their arrival. Backs were slapped and autographs signed, further validation of what they'd just accomplished.

Hanauer rented out one of the hotel ballrooms for friends and family. Gradually, the players were able to peel themselves away from the throng and make their way upstairs. There, one by one, they crashed.

"Like everyone said, it was just a weight lifted off you," Marshall said. "Somehow, my two-year-old daughter was still up, so we kicked it off on the dance floor and got everyone going. Then I just went and sat next to Zach Scott, because I was so tired, and watched people. I had one song in me with the kid, and then I went and sat down with a beer."

Happy clusters dotted the tables, lifelong buddies and spouses and children all sharing in the moment. Over in one of the corners, Frei finally caught a glimpse of the save that offered him Sounders immortality. In the stadium, he hadn't dared look back at the video board as action continued around him. In the immediate aftermath, the MLS Cup MVP was so in demand that he hadn't a spare second in which to collect his thoughts.

Jennifer nudged him with her elbow and pulled up the highlight — *the* highlight — on her phone. The angle from behind the goal in particular was spectacular, giving a sense of how far he'd needed to travel to get to the ball, and how many sinews he'd strained to get his fingertips on it.

"All right, I guess it was decent," Frei acknowledged to his wife, understated as always.

The goalkeeper sat back, took in the scene around him and smiled, content. Few knew just how far he and his teammates had traveled en route to that moment of glory, and when he reclined, the emotions sank in, all at once.

EPILOGUE

THE PARTY DIDN'T LAST long.

As noted, by the time the majority of the Sounders finally left BMO Field, it was past midnight, and the bartenders inside the ballroom stopped serving alcohol at 3 a.m. Most of the players trickled up to their rooms before then, adrenaline wearing off and exhaustion seeping in, not that sleep was easy to come by after all they'd experienced.

Major League Soccer's roster compliance rules required that contract decisions for the following season were due the morning after the title game. That meant that mere hours after the celebratory soiree broke up, exit interviews began taking place in the lobby. The manner was brutal: starting around 8 a.m., Lagerwey, Schmetzer and the rest of the brain trust explained the rationale as to why players who had started in a championship game one day earlier would not be having their contracts renewed for 2017.

The bloodletting was severe. Valdez, Ivanschitz, Friberg and Mears were among those not retained, and both Scott and Gomez would confirm their respective retirements in the coming days. Evans didn't find out for sure whether or not he was sticking around until he landed back at Sea-Tac.

Those conversations were awkward and occasionally strained, completely at odds with the unity among the group just hours earlier. Professional sports, as outlined in more depth earlier on, could be a cruel, cutthroat world.

The flight back to Seattle was thus less raucous than you might imagine. The journey from Colorado and the conference championship was much more triumphant, players going around a circle chanting for one another. (Alonso's botched pronunciation of Scott's last name — "Zach e-Scott" — broke the group into wild fits of laughter.) The charter from Pearson International was quiet in comparison. Guys who were being retained were still riding high from the final, especially the youngsters with less of a sense for their professional mortality. That residual excitement, however, was undercut by fellow passengers with suddenly uncertain futures sitting morosely in window seats.

Hanauer offered to jet his players anywhere they wanted to commemorate the club's first title. Recent NBA champs Golden State and Cleveland had taken to flying straight to Las Vegas to celebrate. Hanauer pitched his team on doing something similar, flying back to Sea-Tac for the parade and then out again to a destination of their choosing, but found few takers.

"We had people from all over the world," Frei said. "I wanted to get the hell out of there. I wanted to go home. It had been an 11-month season. I was done. In retrospect, instead of going from Toronto to Seattle, we should have gone from Toronto straight to Vegas for 24 hours — chilled at every dance club we could find with the shirts on our backs and nothing else — and then gone back to Seattle . . . I guess we'll have to win another one."

They would get the opportunity to make amends for that oversight more quickly — and with far more exact specifications — than anybody on that bittersweet flight back from Toronto could have imagined.

The scale of their achievement hit each of them at different intervals.

Hanauer annually took a postseason trip with his family to a house he owned in Cabo San Lucas, Mexico. The Sounders' fan base was passionate and far-flung enough that he'd usually get a few inquiries about the team on these vacations, or the occasional drink sent his way in gratitude for bringing MLS to Seattle, but this was different. Complete strangers — fellow tourists and waitstaff — excitedly told him they'd watched the championship game and offered their congratulations.

"The clearest memory for me that helped me realize the impact was in December, after the final," Hanauer said. "It made me realize that it wasn't just a local, Seattle thing. Sometimes, when you're born and raised here, sometimes it feels like just a Seattle phenomenon. Having East Coasters or people from Mexico City know about the Sounders, it took me back a little bit and made me realize this has been pretty special."

Frei spent the Monday after the MLS Cup catching up on Twitter. His brother forwarded him articles detailing the reaction from their native Switzerland, and Frei watched videos of his save in a variety of different languages, enjoying the many memes of it making their way around social media.

"During those days, I could scroll [through my notifications] nonstop and never get back to the top, which was cool," Frei said. "I was trying to soak that in."

He and Jennifer spent Christmas Eve at the Dutras', the first time the goalkeeper and his coach could speak at length about the championship. They'd shared an emotional bear hug after Torres buried his PK, but had yet to actually sit down one on one to discuss his standout performance. It was originally a low-key affair, Frei and Dutra sitting on the couch nursing a couple of beers, but it wasn't long before word spread around their neighborhood in Issaquah that the MLS Cup MVP was in their midst.

"All of a sudden I've got like six neighbors coming over, offering me wine, and I know it's because they wanted to see Stef," Dutra said. "That was the real reason."

Frei, forever uncomfortable with attention — "modest and gracious," his coach called him — bashfully bowed his head and mumbled his thanks. It would take time for him to grow into the heroic role he'd unwittingly thrust himself into.

Razov, the assistant coach, cajoled Dempsey into joining him on a friend's bird hunting trip in Eastern Washington a few weeks after the final. The veteran forward's love for the outdoors was renowned, and Razov figured it was a way to get him to open up about having to watch the title run from the sidelines.

One of the most poignant images of the week leading up to the final was the practice at BMO Field the day before the game. While his teammates went through their last-minute preparations, Dempsey was alone down near one of the corner flags doing some light conditioning. At that point, nobody was really sure whether he would ever play again. As his teammates prepared for the biggest game of some of their lives, Dempsey was just beginning the ramp up toward a 2017 return no one was sure would actually happen.

On the hunting trip, Razov got an early indication that Dempsey wasn't ready to call it quits, that if his body cooperated, he still had more to give.

"That kind of led to my getting into his head and seeing what he is all about," Razov said. "Clint is a self-motivator. I think when you have a condition like that, it's a real life-check. It's not a hamstring. It's not a knee. This is something that forces you to take perspective. He was dealing with something that was incredibly scary. And I think he wanted to go out on his terms."

By mid-February 2017, halfway through training camp, Dempsey was officially, medically cleared to return to game action. The 34-year-old minted his first game back with the U.S. national team with a hat trick against Honduras in a World

Cup qualifier in March, eventually going on to tie Donovan for the USMNT's all-time career scoring record. He surpassed all expectations with the Sounders, as well, being named the 2017 MLS Comeback Player of the Year after tallying 12 goals and five assists in 29 league appearances.

Schmetzer was never really able to fully unplug and reflect on that whirlwind few months. He got a few days alone with Kristine in January after the holiday visits from their kids, but otherwise, the grind never really stopped. Especially given the heavy roster turnover — and the fact that Schmetzer had never before coached a full season at the MLS level — attention immediately shifted from winning the championship to defending it.

Less than six weeks after parading the MLS Cup trophy through downtown Seattle streets, the Sounders reported for training camp on a typically dreary, gray January morning at Starfire.

Compared with the campaign that preceded it, 2017 went pretty much according to plan. There was very little drama: no power struggle rumbling beneath the surface, no coaching change, few ego clashes in a locker room that had settled into a defined hierarchy the year before.

In deference to the shortened off-season, Schmetzer was open about his plans to ease his veterans back into form. He warned that such a strategy might lead to a slow start, but few teams in MLS history were as aware that they could flip the switch sometime in the summer and still be OK. So it came to pass. Despite winning just one of their first six games and losing three straight in early May, the Sounders hit their stride around the 4th of July and never looked back.

Lagerwey ably remade the roster around the edges, trading for reliably consistent forward Will Bruin and adding key ancillary pieces to the bottom end of the starting lineup and general rotation. Having Dempsey back healthy and productive certainly helped. Roldan was a revelation, continuing his rapid rise into one of the very best young American prospects.

Otherwise, Seattle was solid if unspectacular. Lodeiro was less effective in his first full season in MLS, teams bodying him out of his comfort zone. Morris, Alonso and Evans spent most of the season banged up — Evans was shuffled out of town after the season, severing one of the final few links to that formative 2009 squad. Still, in a down West and bolstered by one of the stingiest back lines in the league, that was enough to earn the No. 2 seed and a bye straight into the conference semifinals.

Off the field, too, metrics continued a modest but steady rise. They hadn't dramatically spiked with the championship, as the most bullish might have hoped, but they'd charted back upward after the negative blip experienced during the summer of 2016. Group ticket sales were up, Hanauer said, as were corporate renewals. Premium match-day experiences were on the rise, and both merchandise and TV ratings had held steady.

"Hard to say specifically that it is related to a championship," Hanauer said, but it certainly didn't hurt. "To a lot of people in the fan base and inside the organization, and to me personally, it felt like a weight was lifted. The expectations were so high that it just felt like that pinnacle of Major League Soccer had been reached. It burst the balloon of pressure, I think, which has made it more fun for everybody involved, which I think is a good thing for having even more and more success.

"I do think it was important. We definitely wanted to check that box."

One way to measure the weight of their first championship was how freely Seattle played down the stretch run of the 2017 season and during the playoffs. In previous postseasons, the pressure it felt was obvious, previous letdowns infused into present-day performances. As expectations had risen year after year, so the Sounders seemed to be wound tighter and tighter.

That was no longer the case. After Dempsey vanquished Vancouver with a pair of second-half goals in the decisive leg of the conference semifinals, the Sounders steamrolled Houston 5–0 on aggregate to lock up a second consecutive MLS Cup appearance. Waiting on the other side was an intimate foe.

Toronto FC was on the brink of completing the greatest single season in MLS history. Inspired by their near-miss setback the previous December, TFC racked up more regular-season points than any team ever had, earning the right to host another final. The Reds, who'd won the Canadian Championship and the Supporters' Shield, were one victory away from becoming the first side to ever win three major trophies in one calendar year.

To get there, they would need to face off with the team they believed had stolen their rightful crown. If Seattle was going to go back-to-back, it was going to have to return to BMO Field and do it all again on enemy turf.

Narratively, one couldn't have written a better script.

The flight back to Pearson was much more cheerful than the one heading the other way less than a year earlier.

Though Toronto entered the match as deserved favorite given its regular-season exploits, it had looked much less sure of itself during the playoffs. Seattle, meanwhile, swaggered into the final.

The Sounders' portion of the pregame press conferences featured no shortage of inside jokes and shared chuckles between Schmetzer, Frei and Dempsey, of all people. The grizzled, bearded veteran even waxed a little poetic, by his standards, about what it meant for him to be able to come back to Toronto with a chance to play for a championship rather than be marooned up in a luxury box.

"You do appreciate it a little bit more," Dempsey said. "But I've always kind of been somebody who hasn't taken things for granted. I'm happy with what I've been able to accomplish and there's more work to be done."

So much of the 2017 MLS Cup final itself inspired déjà vu. The prematch buildup at BMO Field was just as raucous, if not even more so, than it was the December previous. "O Canada" from the home crowd brought similar chills to the fore. The temperature wasn't quite as frosty — thank god for the late-afternoon kickoff time — but it certainly wasn't balmy.

Just as in the 2016 final, TFC controlled the game but struggled to turn that dominance into an actual goal. For an hour, Frei was on track for a repeat MVP award following a series of increasingly outlandish saves. The building was filled with a here-we-go-again sense of dread. For a few fateful minutes there, it felt as though the Sounders were doing it again, weathering body blows and just waiting for an opening for a sucker punch.

This performance, though, was sloppier. They weren't executing a game plan — for once in his magical year and a half, Schmetzer's Midas touch betrayed him, and his strategy was ill advised — as much as just riding their luck.

It ran out in the 67th minute, when Altidore galloped up the seam onto a perfectly timed Giovinco pass and finished past a stranded Frei. Seattle barely even managed to rouse itself down a goal; it didn't huff and puff so much as wheeze for 15 minutes or so before Victor Vazquez buried the dagger late in stoppage time. The final score was 2–0 for the hosts, but it easily could have been three, four or five if not for Frei's early exploits. The Sounders wandered off the field, heads bowed, while Toronto reveled in its own transformative breakthrough.

The scene in the visiting locker room afterward was almost cruel in its familiarity.

Everything was the same, yet so, so different. Clumps of discarded athletic tape and sod littered the floor rather than crushed celebratory beer cans. No protective tarp over the lockers was necessary. Instead of an impromptu dance party, the players mostly kept to themselves in their respective stalls, spirits downcast and eyes watery.

"You feel like you let down a whole city," Roldan said. "You feel like you let down yourself, your teammates, your family."

The sting would fade with time, but it was sharpened by the realization of just how close they'd come to a rare accomplishment. There was the sense of a fleeting, precious opportunity missed. Only three teams in MLS history — 1996–97 D.C., 2006–07 Houston and 2011–12 Los Angeles — had ever gone back-to-back, a shortlist Seattle couldn't join for at least another two years. Even if it were to somehow get back and win two more, three more consecutive titles, 2017 would always be the one that got away, the missing piece of a potential dynasty.

Plus few understood more acutely than the players themselves how much hard work and good luck goes into reaching a championship game, let alone winning it.

The journey to the brink of back-to-back that began nearly two years earlier claimed a beloved coach, led to institutional turmoil and cost the roster a host of respected veterans who were culled in pursuit of a repeat. The Sounders felt all of it that night in Toronto, an evening so similar and yet so disparate to the one the year before.

In some ways, their 2017 defeat underscored just how special their 2016 triumph had been. So many moving pieces had fallen into place, so many bounces directly into their path, en route to glory. Sometimes, once-in-a-lifetime seasons are just that.

Behind the scenes, the Sounders would continue to grow and strive. Their grand plans remained as ambitious as ever. They wouldn't get to celebrate a repeat, but you never forget your first.

If they are ever to challenge the world's great clubs, history will hold a fond place for that fateful night on the shores of Lake Ontario, when Seattle beat back the odds and lived up to a destiny it had long claimed as its own.

ACKNOWLEDGMENTS

THAT THERE ARE SO many people to thank is a testament to how lucky I am in both my career and my life to be surrounded by such a strong support system. That starts with my parents, Glenn and Cindy, and my little brother, Taylor, all of whom have encouraged me to pursue my dreams. This book certainly qualifies, and it never would have come together without their reassurance during the hard parts.

This book would have never seen the light of day without my editor at ECW, Michael Holmes. As much as soccer has grown in North America, it is still a risky proposition when seeking a mainstream audience. He believed both in this idea and in this first-time author, and I am so grateful for the opportunity.

I have so many friends and colleagues — the fact that that line is so blurred is another mark of my good fortune — who deserve a shout-out for their advice and support throughout this process. That group includes but is not limited to: Grant Wahl, Jayson Jenks, Evan Bush, Mike Gastineau, Larry Stone, Robert Andrew Powell, Stacy Rost, Paige Cornwell, Caitlin Murray, Joel Petterson, Molly Yanity, Jacob Thorpe, Bill Dow, Ryan Horlen and Amanda Snyder.

A sincere thank you to everyone who contributed their time and expertise to this project, including: Sigi Schmid, Garth Lagerwey, Adrian Hanauer, Chris Henderson, Brian and Kristine Schmetzer, Gary Wright, Tom Dutra, Dave Tenney, Kurt Schmid, Ezra Hendrickson, Ante Razov, Stefan and Jennifer Frei, Jordan Morris, Cristian Roldan, Nicolas Lodeiro, Brad Evans, Herculez Gomez, Lamar Neagle, Osvaldo Alonso, Clint Dempsey, Chad Marshall, Nelson Valdez, Chad Barrett, Tyrone Mears, Myron Samuel, Landon Donovan, Kasey Keller, Alan Hinton, Frank MacDonald, Claudia Best, Pete Fewing, Pam Copple, Darren Eales, Carlos Bocanegra, Bob Lenarduzzi, Jason Kreis, Taylor Twellman and Marcus Hahnemann. A special shout out to Sounders press officers Alex Caulfield and Matt Winter for their help in facilitating so much of this.

I also want to thank the *Seattle Times*, especially former and current sports editors Paul Barrett, Don Shelton and Bill Reader, for taking a chance on a young, unproven journalist. It was there that the seeds that would later sprout to become this book were planted, and for that I am forever grateful.

And thanks, finally, to you, the reader — for making it this far and for buying this book in the first place. I have been amazed during these past few years how much folks are willing to go above and beyond to support local writers. Please know that it's not taken for granted, and that this passion project would have never made it all the way to the finish line without your support, too.